BACK
TO LOVE

DENISE JAMES

This is a work on non-fiction and parts of this book has been fictionalised for purpose of a narrative.

Copyright © Denise James 2020

1st Edition, MONTH 2020

Book Design by www.bodhi-design.co.uk

ISBN 978-1-913479-55-8 (paperback)

ISBN 978-1-913479-56-5 (ebook)

Published by That Guy's House

www.ThatGuysHouse.com

Contents

INTRODUCTION

***It is easier to build strong children than to repair broken men.* Frederick Douglass**

This book, *Back to Love*, was born first out of a desire to share a journey, and second to tell a story. The story is one of an abused and abandoned child, and the things that can be done in the dark to such a child, casting a menacing shadow across the child's life when grown; oftentimes for generations to come, if the healing remains undone.

In the telling of this story, my story, the unhealed baton finishes with me, which also makes Back to Love a book about the process of change and its particular twists and turns. It is a self-transformation life story about the not-altogether-straightforward cycle of change, and the coming into being of a more whole and integrated self.

This book was a very difficult book to write. The baring of one's heart and soul, and tortures and loves, in such an open and now public way took me right out of myself, stretching me beyond all measure, on every level. I don't know if I'd call the writing of this book a 'therapeutic' endeavour, but it was certainly an endeavour, to be a true, clear and no-nonsense voice for the most vulnerable in society, that I'd gladly do again and again, however much it hurts.

I don't just speak for the needs of today's children; I speak especially for all the wounded, denied and abandoned children that still exist within countless adults the world over. I write in service to them, as well as to the child within myself. It is my hope that in doing so, we as a society will come to listen more and better respond to children's particular and unique needs and wants, lest those cries turns into screams of blue murder; the kind see and read about on the news and in the papers, daily.

It can also be said that when I speak of the 'child within,' as well as without, I am essentially speaking about the spirit of that first innocent essence; the loving protection, cultivation and bringing forth of which creates emotionally mature, wholesome human beings.

Contrary to popular belief, we are not so much in and of ourselves human beings, but rather it's the case that with the right kind of love, encouragement, modelling and engagement, we grow into that particular skin. We need each other and are bound to each other for our very survival as a species, moving towards an evolution that is benevolent and has no end.

This book spans twenty-three years and tells of the initial and subtle stirrings of change, the definite decision to change, the process of change and what all of that came to entail for me. The reason it is called *Back to Love* is because it has been written for those who, like my past self, do not know due to early, out-of-shaping traumatic experiences that they themselves are the very love they seek. *Back to Love* also talks about the journey from outside-in to inside-out, and then back around the cycle again. This book has been written with heart, for the love of all: *all who have Soul.*

This book has also been written for the everyday, ordinary people – and for *you:* wherever my story finds you on this journey called life. It is my hope that through reading about my own process of change, and my *return* to my *most true self,* that you may realise your own true capacity, and in so doing bring to resolution all obstructions that lay within, in front of and behind of you. As you embark upon this journey, may we, as Henri David Thoreau urged, ***Move more confidently in the direction of your dreams, and dare to live the life Imagined.***

Amongst other things, I am a British-born black woman of African-Caribbean descent, who refused to be a 'statistic' and dared to live the life I imagined growing up, knowing in my heart that life was out there for the taking. May our missing voice in the historical, academic and research records be heard clearly and undeniably here within these pages. May we continue to rise up out of the personal and collective wreckage of traumatised presenting past lives, and like the phoenix continue homeward bound to the places, spaces and lives to which we most belong.

I write in service to you all and hope that in the sharing of this harrowing, and absolutely worthwhile Heroine's Journey, your heart and soul receives the nourishment and encouragement that it needs to embark upon a similar corner-turning journey, if that is your wish; or if your journey has already begun, to continue on with more self-confidence and embodied empowerment.

As the above quote says,

It is easier to build strong children than to repair broken men.

Yes it is easier, but it is not impossible to turn our lives around and drive it in a direction more of your choosing, as my story bares testimony to. I am here, and my Life Purpose is to share the Good News that, with self/love, all things are indeed possible!

Peace, Love & Light,

Denise Marcia James (May 2020)

BOOK ONE:

THE BEGINNING OF ENDS

CHAPTER ONE

The Journey Of A Thousand Miles Begins With A Single Step. Lao Tzu

The decision to have a child changed my life forever. The year was 1982, and I was seventeen-and-a-half years old. I could have done much better in school the previous year, but looking back, circumstance didn't really allow it. The only lesson I really enjoyed was Sociology, as it was the only subject that seemed relevant to real life; the only subject that attempted to decipher and understand it, a thing that was very important to me.

When I left school that summer with my one 'O' Level, I was not at all sure what I wanted to do in regard to a career. None of the adults around me at this time were available to actively explore that side of things with me, and so it was more or less left up to me and the school to decide what my future would look like. During the summer break, I half-heartedly decided to enrol on a two-year Community Studies course. I thought that a course in the caring professions would best suit me, especially if it involved working with children. I loved taking care of children.

To begin with, the course did hold my attention. The college was newly-built and I enjoyed the experience of being part of a new endeavour and a new group. I also enjoyed the new relationship that was to be had with teachers – more equal, friendly and respectful – and I really liked the course tutor, Leila. She was warm, cuddly and motherly. I also liked the fact that being at college was entirely my own affair, which gave me a sense of freedom that I enjoyed.

However, at times that freedom, that responsibility, brought with it a foreboding cloud of uncertainty and feelings of insecurity, especially about the future. Where would the future lead me? Would it take me to very difficult places, like my past had? These fears, which were more unconscious at the time, scared and overwhelmed me, so much so that by the end of the first year, my enthusiasm began to wane, bringing with it a loss of concentration, and not long afterwards absolute boredom. It was an old, familiar angst-filled boredom, and resultant dissociation, born out of extreme dissatisfaction, that often saw me falling asleep during lessons.

I quite enjoyed those little naps, though it was of great embarrassment to me when Leila pulled me up on it. She was concerned that I wasn't enjoying the course anymore, and wondered if there was something else that would better hold my attention. But, as bored as I was, and as lost as I felt at times, there wasn't really any other place during the day where I felt relatively safe and could comfortably be, let alone peacefully fall asleep. So, I tried my hardest not to sleep in class, but it continued to be a struggle.

The only subjects that kept my full attention were those to do with childcare and development. It was during these lessons that certain ideas began to come to mind, and, I guess, started to better fill the uncomfortable spaces of my time. Those thoughts pertained to the desire to become a mother and have a child, *all of my own.*

In hardly any time at all, I found myself acting on those ideas, an endeavour I gave body, mind and soul to, and one which brought with it renewed hope and anticipated joy. The idea that I could have a child to love, and to love me in return, made me feel so totally happy, and gave a new lease to what felt and seemed at the time to be a life going nowhere, slow.

Essentially, I made the decision alone, since alone I often was. I had been with my boyfriend Ronald for about 5 months. He was my first true, obsessive love. I was besotted with him, but also painfully aware that he was not meeting my needs, or wants, for that matter. I was aware that the relationship wasn't at all secure, which only served to intensify the need – my need at the time – for something more.

By then, my childhood had come to an abrupt and bitterly disappointing end, bringing with it the full realisation that my mother was never going to give me the love and security I needed. My mother went abroad frequently. The day she left again, I was seventeen-and-a-half years old and only just with child. Perhaps being pregnant helped cushion the blow of her latest departure. We wouldn't see her again for another five years.

I was totally overjoyed at being pregnant, an experience that went some way towards eliminating varying degrees of sadness and loneliness – emotional states that had been a concrete part of my felt reality for as long as I could remember. It wasn't that those difficult and painful states completely disappeared, but for a time, they no longer disturbed me in the same old ways. For his part, especially considering that I hadn't given him a choice in the matter, Ronald didn't seem to mind my being pregnant, which made me doubly happy. To me, that meant the child was wanted by both of us, and so we carried on.

When my absolutely gorgeous baby boy was born 20th March 1983, at 7.40pm, weighing in at 6lbs 13oz, words could not express the absolute joy I felt in my heart and within my very being, even though moments before I'd been having what felt like serious second thoughts! I had been in labour since the previous evening, when my waters had broken without contractions. The nurses had inserted a tablet to help induce contractions to no avail, and so I had been placed on a drip and started off first thing the following morning. It had been a hard labour.

However the joy in my heart immediately eclipsed the pain as soon as I met my beautiful son, Jamie. He had these bright, deeply-set and oval-shaped eyes, like mine, a perfect little nose and curly black hair; features that, in the beginning, oftentimes caused him to be mistaken for a little girl. He was a most wonderful, remarkable work of art, if I do say so myself, and not too long after his arrival, in the secret chambers of my heart, I promised to give him all that I never had, but had desperately needed and had sought as a child. I vowed to both him and myself that this would be my second chance, and for him, the best of possible starts.

Needless to say, I didn't complete the Community Studies course, though I managed to get another 'O' Level under my belt, this time in English Literature. I was very proud of that!

I'd moved in with my sister right before giving birth to Jamie, due to our family home becoming overrun with mice. We'd had a problem with mice for some years, but as my mother had become increasingly absent, a certain degree of hygiene had gone out the window, and when my two older sisters, Beverly and Terri left to start their own lives, the situation got ten-times worse.

The kitchen was the worst. It became a place where, after a time, no one dared enter, let alone attempt to cook in or store food. That room also carried the mice's awful smell more than any other, although the rest of the house wasn't too far behind. Additionally, the fridge had long since broken down and subsequently developed a unique smell of its own. To this day, I can't stand mice; I can't see one without filling up with dread; I cannot see one without feeling the feelings I was unable to feel then, being frozen, for mere survival.

I was glad to be staying at Beverly's, as it had been ever so lonely being pregnant and predominantly alone in that mice-infested house. My sister Lauren was always out from dusk 'til dawn, and Ronald had visited and stayed whenever he could. I hadn't minded that too much because I used to feel so embarrassed and ashamed when he stayed, especially on nights when, in the stillness, the mice seemed to make so much noise.

By the by, staying with Beverly was OK, especially when I first came home from hospital with my beautiful baby boy. They, my sisters, had obviously gone out of their way to make sure that the room I was to share with my brother Curtis was just right. It was warm, inviting and cosy, with a cot bought, set up, and everything. It seemed like a proper little nest, and I felt well taken care of, for which I was extremely grateful.

After a couple of months living with Beverly I decided to I put my name down on the council waiting list for a flat, and was overjoyed when, three months after giving birth, I received a temporary offer of accommodation in a bedsit for new parents. The bedsit had only recently been opened, and was just up the road from Beverly's. And two months later, I was even more overjoyed to receive an offer of a flat to call my own.

I truly enjoyed my time in the bedsit, relishing the whole experience of going it totally alone. Having my own space in my own place was such a big deal for me; it was a dream come true, and one that I took to, i.e. being a homemaker, like a duck to water, much as I had motherhood. I made some good – then and there- friends in the bedsit, which had a real community vibe, but although I was sad to leave, I was so looking forward to moving into my new flat.

BOOK ONE:

THE BEGINNING OF ENDS

CHAPTER TWO

Running a house was very challenging in places, particularly financially. In that regard, the experience of setting up a home was a bit disillusioning. I was on benefits, £38-a-week, and everything; shopping, bills, clothes etc. had to come out of that. I would get my money on a Monday, and by Wednesday it would be all gone. It was a real struggle. I had to do without on so many different levels, which at times made me quite depressed. I was still young, wanting and needing so much, all of which now, once again, seemed well out of reach.

Even though Ronald worked full-time as a sales assistant in a shoe shop, he wasn't properly living with me, and because deep down I felt so undeserving and unsure of exactly where I stood with him, I found it really hard to ask him for any kind of help. With regard to Jamie I had expected Ronald to do better, since he came from a seemingly more stable family background, with a traditional home where his mum and dad were together and married; a home where the father worked while the mother stayed at home, very much at the centre of her children's upbringing.

In regards to parenting styles, Ronald tended to err on the side of total complacency by way of not wanting to upset Jamie, giving into his wants and whims and failing to discipline him in any way, which sometimes set me up as the bad guy when I tried to put in place basic routines, rules and boundaries. On the other hand, from the time Jamie was born until he was three years old, father and son had enjoyed a beautiful bond. They had been close; they had played together and Ronald had been openly affectionate towards him. For the sake of Jamie's optimal psychological and emotional development, I had been very pleased by that.

The other major difficulty that I experienced in setting up my new home was the way that my social life seemed to pack up. I used to like clubbing, but I wasn't able to go out when I wanted to because it was difficult finding babysitters. Our mother gave us a lot of freedom growing up, and as a family we were always affiliated with the music scene in one way or another. My mother loved music; she was a connoisseur of vintage reggae, revival and soul, and had a record collection to die for. She could have easily given the various DJs and Sound Men at the time a run for their money.

I used to get so jealous of a friend with whom I had shared my pregnancy. We got pregnant around the same time, and no, we didn't plan it that way. She had her mother around, so unlike me, she was never stuck when it came to wanting to go out or just generally getting help. In my new home, on those needing, wanting and skint Saturday nights, and especially when Ronald was out, which was often, I once again found myself feeling very alone and believing that I was missing out.

Financially, things began to improve in 1985 when I applied and successfully became a registered childminder. Being in a more financially secure position was a new experience for me, and it was nice not having to struggle or worry about making ends meet. At times, I didn't know how to spend the money. I was earning £150-a-week, which was a big deal for me.

Another major improvement, occurring around six months after I moved into the flat, was that Ronald appeared to have changed. We seemed to have settled into being more of a family together, and things were relatively happy. I say relatively, because when Ronald and I first started going out there was a rumour that he was still seeing his former girlfriend, Norma. I assumed that she was out of the picture shortly after Jamie was born and I had heard through the grapevine that she was pregnant by someone else. However, I still felt that I could not relax in the relationship, just in case.

My insecurities had started on the evening we met when I was a naïve sixteen-and a half year-old. Ronald was a good-looking and popular guy and I couldn't for the life of me understand why he had chosen to be with me.

After about a year of what seemed like matrimonial bliss, with Ronald staying in more, us going out together on occasion, and basically him, Jamie and me enjoying more quality time in doors, things began to change. By then, we had been together for nearly five years. I had been counting because I was so happy to still be with my 'baby father,' something that was really important to me. Sadly infidelity rumours began again.

Ronald became moody and uninvolved. He raved almost every night of the week, and just couldn't relax or be still. Then, one night, while I was at one of his dances helping out behind the bar, along with my sisters and a few other family friends, I just couldn't for the life of me shake this uneasiness I had felt immediately upon arriving. I was so aware of it, but in the end, I put it down to me being me, for I often felt very nervous and self-conscious when I went out, especially if Ronald was about, and only dancing could remedy it. However, the feeling I had was something more than just that typical insecurity.

I remained in the bar for about an hour , and then decided to go upstairs and have a little dance. It was very difficult for me to be around what I consider to be good music and not give in to the need to start dancing. I was only in the room for about ten minutes before I began to feel extremely uncomfortable, like I was being watched. I turned to the left and immediately met my observer's gaze. I knew in an instant that it was Jennie.

Like I said, I had been hearing rumours, recent ones, and one of the girls mentioned was Jennie. My neighbour's friend had informed me that she and Ronald had been seen out together on a number of occasions, and that they were most definitely an item. I had also received information that she was a pretty young thing of mixed parentage.

It had truly hurt me to hear those things, but I already had a way of dealing with 'hurt.' When it came to Ronald, if I was hurt, I would first become incensed, wanting to immediately seek him out and find out the whole truth. He would always deny everything, arguing that the people telling me these lies were small-minded and jealous, and just trying to break us up. Then I would begin to doubt myself and my feelings, wondering if perhaps he was right and questioning people's motives for telling me in the first place. I would then put it all mentally away someplace through escaping with a binge eating/purging exercise. I was Bulimic, and I had been since the age of fourteen.

On that night, however, I would find out the truth from the horse's mouth; a truth that she was more than willing to share with me. She also added a few new details to the story; a miscarriage, the actual days, nights and times she had seen Ronald and how he'd told her we weren't together. All of that was quite apart from another new and current affair with a girl named Susan, which he had denied to Jennie.

I was in a total daze. I was in absolute shock and feeling more insecure about myself than ever, not least because Jennie was so pretty and so very well turned out, looking like she'd never wanted for anything. However, along with these feelings, I also felt a rage, a rage I had never known before. It was a rage that gave me strength and confidence; one that directed me knowingly, and which I sensed could very easily cause certain damage. It was powerful and noticeable, especially for someone like me: sweet, good girl, a peace-maker.

After I had finished talking to Jennie, I left the room and went directly next door, where Ronald was. Luckily for him, that room wasn't full, and in the coolness of a rare clarity, strength and rage, I told him what I had just learned. He remained silent; he didn't appear to know what to say.

I could tell how different I was being, and the totally unnerving effect that was having on him; he hadn't met this side of me before; indeed, I had never met this side of me before. Then, I said to him, "Give me back my fucking keys!" which he did immediately. I could see a certain terror in his eyes; he was like a little boy being chastised, fearful he would soon get a beating, or worse still, be shamed in front of all these people, people that he was so keen to please and gain the approval of. I didn't allow myself to make a great big scene, however, regardless of how tempting it was.

After I'd snatched my keys from him, I left the room and went outside, where I sat on a wall and tried hard to hold back the tears that had started to replace the rage. An old friend from the rave scene came over, as he could see how upset I was despite how much I was trying not to show it. He tried to cheer me up, but it was no use. I just left without saying goodbye to anybody.

By the time I got home, the rage had returned again in full force. I so wanted to hurt him, to get him back, and his precious clothes came to mind first. His persona was far more real than he was, and I knew this would hit him where it hurt; he loved his clothes, his appearance and his good looks. Luckily, even though he still wasn't fully living with me, he had a lot of his best clothes there, so very carefully and deliberately, I cut up the best items; those most expensive and dear (Jamaican patois meaning very costly). One-by-one I nipped and tucked, and when I was done, I carefully folded them, making them appear neatly packed and ready for him to pick up from outside the front door, where I left them in bin bags.

We broke up, our first proper separation. Sadly, and

unfortunately, Jamie had witnessed his departure and had got really upset about it, begging his daddy not to go. I was so angry at Ronald. I knew he had to go and that I had to take a stand against his cheating ways, but I had forgotten to stop and anticipate the effect it would have on Jamie. I remember feeling so bad for lacking the foresight to have packed Jamie off somewhere, so that he would not have had to witness our quarrelling and his father leaving. It was truly heart-breaking.

At one point, I remember being outside on the balcony as Ronald collected the last of his belongings, and I looked him straight in the eyes and asked, "How am I ever going to love again?" I had loved him so much, and my heart broke further again when my neighbour later informed me that Ronald had also been affected enough to cry; she had seen him.

The break-up lasted just under a month. It was very hard, especially when Ronald came to take Jamie out. Seeing him on those occasions truly tested my resolve, and when he started making subtle innuendos that later became advances, I decided to write him a letter. In it, I expressed the full range of my feelings, especially how disappointed and hurt I had been. I also told him that I would only be prepared to take him back if he promised to finish with Jennie.

In response to the letter he came around and we kind of talked, and he kind of did and didn't make any promises in regard to Jennie and our future together. Somehow, though, the need to not be alone, and to believe in him and us, as well as my familiar story of accepting, settling and making the best out of peanut affection, outweighed the need to protect myself and walk away.

So, we became on again, although all trust had been totally shattered; there was no denying that. The other name, the Susan person, remained in the background, unquestioned and unconfirmed, whilst I contended with childminding, making home improvements and enjoying my darling, precious little boy. And when things got really bad, especially in the way of painful and difficult unresolved feelings resurfacing, I still had my little friend Bulimia, however destructive her ways.

BOOK ONE:

THE BEGINNING OF ENDS

CHAPTER THREE

Ronald continued not to change. He just couldn't or wouldn't commit, and even though someplace I knew it, I also couldn't or wouldn't see it, let alone deal with it head on. Somehow, I kept believing and working under the premise that if I tried harder and proved how much I loved him, that he would eventually love and commit to me in return; that he would finally see what a good, understanding, forgiving and caring person I was and had been; that he would finally SEE ME and love me and accept me the way I so desperately needed.

As I endeavoured to carry on with Ronald's good efforts that never lasted long, I began to feel increasingly out of my depth, which was a feeling I hadn't experienced before. In my life up to that point, it had become extremely important for me to feel that I had a certain degree of control over my feelings; my very (daily) survival seemed to depend on it. Now, with all that was going on between Ronald and I, my precarious well-being became threatened, which by the same token made everything begin to feel on the brink of becoming terribly out of control. This was terrifying to me.

My thought processes were beginning to break down. I couldn't think things through as clearly as I once did, and solutions began to elude me. I feared that I was losing my mind, which had been my place of solace and comfort. At the time, I was also trying to maintain a level of resolve when it came to refraining from eating certain foods, namely one, two, three or four packets of crisps at a time, but more and more I would find myself comfort eating – binging and purging to numb the pain. I was washing the forbidden food all down and away with an ever-increasing number of laxatives in order to avoid putting weight on, lest I reveal myself as the needy, greedy, fat and undeserving person I secretly felt that I was. Every morning I'd wake up hating myself, especially when I thought about the physical harm that I was doing to my body by abusing it in this way.

Then, I would resolve to once again start afresh, after which I'd make a certain amount of progress until the stress and pressure and the emotional pain built up and I'd inevitably find myself back at square one. That was how the cycle would go, getting even more desperate and destructive than before. Previously, the binge eating and subsequent purging had been somewhat under my control, as I would only have an episode perhaps two or three times a week, and occasionally I'd even miss a week altogether. However, at this point it was almost every day and sometimes more than once.

During this time, my sleeping also became disturbed, and another place where I found solace was denied as night after night sleep brought me dreams of Ronald treating me even more badly than he did in my waking life. It was almost as if my subconscious, my very soul, was in its own way trying to wake me up and get me to SEE the destruction that my relationship with Ronald was havocking upon me. I truly felt that I was going crazy during those four months, so much so that I began to have grave concerns as to where it would all lead; how it would all end.

My dream of a happy family was unravelling before my very eyes. I could no longer see a clear and hopeful ending, or at least not with Ronald. I couldn't sustain the phantasy any longer, and I worried about the effect that Ronald and I continuing on in this vein would have on Jamie, both in the long- and short-term; especially the ramifications of me potentially losing control of my faculties.

I didn't want Jamie to have the experience of that kind of mother, an outcome which for me would have been the ultimate nightmare. Besides, that wasn't the promise I had made to him or to us. His being in the world was meant to be a second chance, and so one grey and cold October morning, after awakening out of another series of bad dreams following another night of binge eating, I decided to make an appointment to see my GP.

I arrived for my appointment at the doctor's office feeling somewhat anxious and ashamed, like I was making-mountains-out-of-mole hills. The doctor was white, more than middle-aged and very much upper-class, and when he gave the 'what seems to be the problem' line, I blurted it all out before I could change my mind.

I mentioned feeling a loss of control, my inability to think straight, the bad indigestion I was now experiencing, a growing unhappiness, despair and the awful nightmares. I left out the tiny, major detail of the bulimia, as well as Ronald's infidelities. For some reason, the sharing of these two issues felt out-of-bounds, and not allowed.

The doctor listened, and when I was through, he told me that it sounded like I was depressed and experiencing a nervous breakdown. He asked some more questions , and then went on to prescribe a course of anti-depressants and sleeping tablets, encouraging rest and relaxation. That was it. When I left Dr's office, I felt ever-so excited and relieved, as going to see him had not been a waste of time after all. Something was really wrong; something that had a name... nervous breakdown; depression...

I felt a sense of validation that, somewhere deep inside, I knew had been a very long time coming. My inner unhappiness had finally been acknowledged, and I felt elated. Being a bit of a bookworm, it wasn't long before I was down the local library seeking out additional information, and possible remedies, for the aforementioned conditions, which brought me into contact with a book by Wayne Dyer, *Erroneous Zones*, which would be a life-changing read for me. It was the book that truly set me on the path of self-recovery; that helped me turn a certain corner emotionally at a very painful and difficult time in my life.

Feeling almost as if vision had been restored, I got myself 'on-side' again, and committed to not only raising my son right, but also to working towards a certain recovery for myself. As luck, or providence, would have it, a week after visiting the doctor I came upon an article in a women's magazine on the subject of eating disorders.

After reading the article in almost a 'time-standing-still' trance, I once again felt jubilation. The article left me feeling further validated, understood and inspired; there was actually a name for what I did with food. It was called Bulimia, and it was a problem that I shared with many others. It was also something that, with the right help, could be treated and dismantled, and help was at hand at the bottom of the page, through the Women's Therapy Centre.

As soon as I'd finished reading the article, I made contact with the centre and learned that help would come in the form of a weekly therapy group for women with troubled relationships with food. I was also told that if I fitted the criteria and was indeed interested, I could leave my details and they would get in touch to arrange a consultation. I did just that.

I didn't take the pills that the doctor prescribed me for long, the reason being that I'd found the sleeping pills to take away a certain quality from the experience of sleep, namely my dreams. Also, the anti-depressants that I was told would take a couple of weeks or so to kick in didn't seem to be doing the trick, and I had become impatient and couldn't be bothered to wait and see. Plus, I had felt at the time that it had seemed unreasonable and unrealistic for me to rely solely on a bottle of pills to make things right, there were reasons behind the depression, and so after about two and a half weeks I just stopped taking them both, and instead eagerly awaited my consultation for the Eating Disorder

Therapy Group.

That's how I saw out the year of 1986. A year that had been quite traumatic overall was ending on the note of hope. So at the start of 1987 I was feeling pretty good and things were still looking very hopeful. I had also been for the eating disorder therapy consultation and received the good news that I had been accepted into the group, which met on a weekly basis for an hour and a half, every Monday for six months. Initially, the group had started off with six members before it grew to eight, but by the last two months it had dwindled down to just two. In the final month there remained just the two therapists and I, which was very difficult to deal with, bringing with it painful old feelings.

There were feelings of disappointment and fear; the main fear being that because I had become much more visibly open, weepy and vulnerable in sessions, I'd somehow scared off Gilly, who'd been the last girl standing. There was also disappointment because I had been given the strong impression as a child that to display one's feelings was totally unacceptable, unbearable and burdening, implying that I ought to deny them, stop being a cry-baby and be strong instead. I grew up feeling most decidedly ashamed of my feelings, especially the more vulnerable ones.

Still, the experience of therapy helped immensely. It helped me put things into perspective, and also helped me to understand that my childhood had been far from what's considered 'normal.' I came to understand that my childhood had been quite lacking and neglectful in detrimental ways, and that as such it had negatively impacted my emotional development. I realised that certain childhood experiences had informed and shaped me, and in turn influenced how I felt not only about myself, but also about the world and my place within it.

Fundamentally, therapy helped me to begin to understand how the eating disorder was essentially a symptom of deep-seated problems that originated from particular past traumas, as well as various unmet developmental needs, all of which were still in desperate need of being acknowledged, released and grieved for.

I took a lot from those therapy sessions, even though they got really painful and difficult in places. I wasn't used to sharing my innermost thoughts and feelings with anyone, let alone strangers, but then I also wasn't used to receiving so much understanding, care, support and attention, all of which I lapped up, like the emotionally-starved child I was.

The meeting of these unmet needs to be seen, understood, held in mind, supported and cared about, simply because I exist, blew my mind. This nurturing, therapeutic experience, along with all the insights I was gaining, served to increase my thirst for self-knowledge and self-understanding, and reignited the fire that had begun burning inside of me when I decided to become a mother and find purpose in that life direction.

So, once again I was at the library, reading, reading and reading anything and everything related to eating disorders, female psychology, mental health, identity and relationships. To list but a few: *Fat is a Feminist Issue, Womansize, The Tyranny of Slenderness, The Hungry Heart, Women who Love Too Much, The Cinderella Complex, What Do Women Want?* Alongside all of those, I continued working with the *Erroneous Zone* book that had started me off on this recovery journey. My aim at that time was to become an overall more present moment living, fully-functioning and happy person.

The need to binge and purge began to dissipate. Indeed, four months into the therapy I managed to stop vomiting all together and became more able to keep my food down, even when I felt I had eaten that little bit too much. In the past, this feeling would have most definitely triggered a binge, so this represented a real breakthrough for me. In my wildest of dreams, I hadn't believed that I would have been able to release the hold that having an eating disorder had on me. It had felt so huge and so needed, like a mighty compulsion coming from a deep, dark and very deprived place.

Due to this therapeutic influence, I was beginning to feel a growing inner contentment and peace, brought on by having somewhere to go, to speak, to be heard, to share and to get to truly know and understand myself, especially those underlying, misunderstood feelings. I hadn't been educated in an emotional sense before; being so emotionally fed met the tip of an enormous iceberg.

BOOK ONE:

THE BEGINNING OF ENDS

CHAPTER FOUR

In regard to the traumas I had experienced as a child, there were two key experiences that surfaced in the group, where I saw them in a new light for what they truly were, and realised the life-shaping and almost soul-destroying effect they'd had on me. These related to the sexual abuse I had experienced as a child, as well as the repeated separations experienced due to my mother's constant comings and goings. The two came to be very much related.

The sexual abuse experience made me feel very ashamed, afraid, cut off, alone and even more *different*. I hated it, just as I did all subsequent reoccurrences. It felt disgustingly horrible, and I felt dirty and nasty. Secretly, I wanted to kill him, but it was safer to kill myself; safer to try and instead kill my feelings about it. I had had a lot of experience of killing my feelings by that point in my life.

During therapy, recovering the sexual abuse and naming it for what it was, while also acknowledging the number of separations I had been put through and the resulting sense of overwhelming abandonment it left me with, not least because it had formed the backdrop within which the sexual abuse had taken place, provided me with some pieces of a very large and hazy puzzle.

At the time of the group therapy sessions, my feelings were only just beginning to thaw out, never mind catch up sufficiently with, and go more deeply and thoroughly into, the heart of recovery that was to follow, but at least the work, the journey and the healing had begun. It was also during this time that I decided to broach the subject with my mother, who was due to return home from her five-year stay in America.

My mother had only been back in the country a month or so when I began to experience an urgent desire to share some of my feelings and findings with her, so I wrote her a letter straight from the heart. In the letter, I expressed how unwanted, abandoned and unloved I had felt as a child, generally, as well as during her absences. However, telling her about the sexual abuse hadn't entered my mind at that point.

It was a difficult letter to write, at least in terms of being so open and honest. Letters and phone calls had been the way we'd communicated during her spells away, and because we never had a phone, we would all have to gather around a neighbour's or friends who had one, quickly taking turns to talk. During those times, I always took care to make her feel that she was a good mother and was doing her best by us. I knew this was what she wanted, and indeed needed, to hear.

This letter was different, as it came from someplace else inside of me, and solely on my own behalf. It took care of my feelings, leaving her to take care of her own. It took a lot of guts for me to write, and deep inside, even though I was angry, I was equally or perhaps even more so, terrified of how she would receive it. But receive it I knew she would, as there was no turning back or around for me now.

I had invited my mother round to my flat in the afternoon to talk. She hadn't asked what it was about, nor had I offered to tell her. When she arrived, I made her a cup of tea and then small talk ensued, and once that was out of the way, I told her that I had written a letter and that I wanted to share it with her. I read the letter out; it was the hardest thing I had ever done. It was my hope that she would truly listen and hear me. Instead, once the reading was done, she went straight into defence mode.

All I got from her by way of an explanation was, 'I guess I wasn't thinking,' and in regard to what I thought were tell-tale signs that all was not well – e.g. my being very inhibited, shy, withdrawn, unhappy, terribly nervous and forlorn – she responded by saying that she thought that was just what I was like. She claimed that that was who I was and wanted to be back then, so she just left me to be what she thought was my most natural self and way of being.

That was it; that was like previous letters and phones calls, nothing meaningful was exchanged. Her words felt empty, or at least that's how I received them. I had hoped and wished that there would have been or could have been more, but I was still very glad to have gotten it off my chest. I didn't regret a word of it. These were feelings that I wouldn't get a chance to work through, either, since the therapy group had come to an end. I was back on my own, emotionally further along, but still with some way to go.

BOOK ONE:

THE BEGINNING OF ENDS

CHAPTER FIVE

Outside of therapy, disclosures and confrontations, the spring of 1987 saw me growing increasingly restless in terms of vocation. I was still childminding, but it wasn't satisfying me. I needed and wanted something more; something outside the home. Jamie was three years old at the time, a bright, inquisitive, happy and secure little boy. I had put his name down on the local nursery waiting list, and when he was accepted and later settled in, I decided to quit child minding. Not too long after that, I found and secured for myself a part-time sales assistant job at a local shoe shop.

It wasn't too long before I noticed that money became a little tight again, as I had been earning that bit more as a childminder. However, I did enjoy being out of the house and having more space and time to myself in that way. Circumstances continued to work against the dream of happy families. Ronald still seemed happy enough to have one foot in my door and the other someplace else, which made it feel like we weren't really together; that we were living totally separate lives. It all still felt one-sided, reopening old wounds and making me unable to truly find happiness and peace in the relationship.

Then, the rumours of him cheating on me became rampant again. Jennie's name still remained, and as providence would have it, it wasn't too long – June of that year, in fact – before I bumped into her again. During this encounter, she went on to tell me that they were still together, but that it was on and off because he was also seeing someone else; the Susan girl she had mentioned to me before. She also went on to tell me that not only was Ronald still seeing Susan, but that Susan was pregnant by him and had perhaps already had the baby. It was all a bit too much to take in; the conversation left me stunned, shocked and lost. It all seemed terribly unreal, and I did and didn't want to believe it or have to go through that heartache again.

When I brought it to his attention the very next moment that I saw him, he denied it, which made me feel even more confused and crazy. And because, like I said, a part of me didn't want it to be true, I believed him. *Why would he lie if it were true, but then why would Jennie lie?* I wondered. *Maybe she just had it wrong about Susan – people make mistakes.* However, this time around I was a much stronger person. I still wasn't vomiting or bingeing, which made things, even at this time, still feel quite hopeful for me.

Three weeks after my meeting with Jennie, towards the end of July 1987, I woke one morning feeling ever so restless, and felt immediately compelled to find out the exact truth regarding the

Susan situation once and for all. Ronald not keeping his word to return home the night before made the need to know even more compelling, and my thoughts went to an unnamed telephone number I had copied out of his diary. For some reason, at the time it was like I instinctively knew that writing that number down would one day prove quite useful, and this seemed to be that day. That morning, I retrieved it from under the mattress, where it had been hidden for the past couple of months or so.

Tentatively, I dialled the number. A girl answered, Susan, who went on to tell me all that I needed, but feared, to know. Yes, she was going out with Ronald, and had been for a year and a half now, and yes they'd had a baby, a girl, in June. And by the by, he had told her that he and I were no longer together, and therefore she was shocked and upset to know otherwise.

I ended the conversation with Susan feeling very angry and disillusioned. I felt so devastated, such a fool, immediately calling him at work and letting him have it, whereupon he tried to turn it back onto me by bringing up the time I'd cut up his clothes and chucked him out. This made no sense to me, however, and just seemed absolutely irrelevant to the conversation at hand. I was so fucking mad.

I so wished that I still had the therapy group. There was no one to talk to; nowhere to go and offload. What I did do, though, was contact the Women's Therapy Centre and speak to one of the therapist, briefly, about my situation and desire for further support, and I was so grateful and relieved when they were able to give me the number of other organisations that I could go to for help. One of these was Open Door in Crouch

End, a counselling service for young people between the ages 18-25, which I qualified for, being only twenty-two at the time. I contacted them, and after a consultation secured weekly individual counselling sessions that would start in September of that year and would last for two years; the knowledge of which was very comforting, providing me with a much-needed lifeline.

During the summer of 1987, I inadvertently struck up a close relationship with my sister Beverly's friend, Heather, who was also my fast-becoming-distant friend Marilyn's older sister. Heather and I had shared a connection from around the time when I had not too long started seeing Ronald, and he had (even then) been stressing me out. In want of someone to talk to, I had gone to Marilyn's house and she had been out, so I ended up kind of talking to Heather instead, as I was quite emotional. It wasn't that we quickly became friends, but it was the basis of the initial connection. At the time, and in her own way, Heather had tried to be there for me.

Another connection between Heather and I was plaiting; she would regularly put my hair into extensions and I'd do hers, a thing that had really helped my hair to grow. Sometimes, I'd stay at her house, and that felt doubly good. I loved having someone older to take me in, feed me, enjoy my company and to share a spliff with. I started smoking weed (cannabis) more frequently around that time, having previously taken a puff here and there, but not going any further because it gave me cravings, and therefore made me vulnerable to overeating. However, post-therapy group I noticed that I became a bit better at smoking weed without overdoing it with the cravings. I felt quite good about that.

Weed was easily accessible. Like I said, Heather smoked it and always had some to share, and my family smoked, too, including my mum and dad, and my next-door neighbour's husband Ernie sold it at five pounds a draw. Throughout the Susan situation, and because of my regular liaisons with Heather, I began to smoke it a little bit more, and before long I was buying from Ernie on a regular basis.

Heather would also bring me news from the 'what Ronald is up to now' grapevine, which I did and didn't mind at varying times. We had very obviously broken up following the Susan discoveries. Things had definitely changed.

Having become extremely bored working in the shoe shop, I left, deciding instead to seriously consider returning to education. In regard to a career, I began to feel the need to do something more fulfilling; something that stretched me and could help me further tap into my true capabilities. Intuitively, I knew I needed a challenge, something outside of Ronald, to give my life journey a fresh direction, as well as added meaning. So, in September 1987, a month after the christening ordeal, I applied to do some courses at City and Islington College.

Although my initial thoughts were to perhaps try some individual courses in Sociology, Psychology, and English Language, after discussions with a course tutor at a college opening day, I decided to enrol on the course he was running. This was a part-time access course for mature students wishing to enter higher education, but who did not have the formal entry qualifications required.

It was good having college to not only take my mind off

Ronald, but also give me something unknown and different to look forward to. The idea of meeting more new and interesting people truly excited me, as a lot, if not most, of my girlfriend relationships had seemed to have met a certain end. I had grown apart from them, and them, me: the me. I was discovering and on another level felt like my life was just beginning.

The kind of life I most wanted, that is; the kind of chances that I was still adamant on creating for myself. Still, as the course's start date approached, I had to work really hard against myself, to fight what seemed like an urge to self-sabotage. A feeling of fear was trying to make me do some kind of U-turn; trying to change my mind and make me late by putting so many obstacles in the way the morning of my starting the course, even though *The Way* was clear.

A great big anxiety began growing inside me; one which I didn't quite understand, because at the same time I really wanted to start college; really wanted this something more and something 'new.' I didn't understand at the time how much of a very big step going back into education was for me, and not only that, just how difficult it was also for me to go for what I wanted, and to feel entitled to it. *What if I cannot keep up?* I asked myself. *What if I fail miserably?* I wondered if I'd screw it all up, just like how, in spite of all my efforts, I had failed to create my 'happily ever after' family... *What if... What if... What if...*

These mostly unconscious thoughts and fears awakened old feelings of inadequacy, wrapped tightly in the belief that I didn't deserve good things, and that good things are not for the likes of me. However, knowing that I'd have the individual therapy sessions to accompany and support me on the next leg of my journey comforted me greatly.

BOOK TWO

INSIDE - OUT

CHAPTER ONE

"In the Creative Process, the Order of Life is Inner before Outer," (*source unknown*)

Starting college was difficult at first, but once the anxiety calmed down, I came to see that it wasn't anything I couldn't handle. I came to truly enjoy the whole experience; it was the best move I had made in years. The course focused on particular themes in Psychology and Sociology, as well as research and, more importantly, on the general and specific study skills needed for higher education and academic school life.

The two tutors who ran the course were really nice people; laid back and easy to relate to. I felt a particular, yet at times uneasy, closeness to one of them, and I'm sure he felt something similar towards me. Or then again, perhaps it just felt like something out of the ordinary because I had been so deprived of attention and encouragement, and he made a lot of time for me. He felt that I had interesting ideas, and that I should be more confident about sharing and expressing them, especially in a classroom environment.

But expressing and sharing my ideas in front of the class was a totally nerve-wracking experience, especially the first time I had to it. On that occasion, I had to research and discuss the subject of deviancy; what it means and how it had been perceived in the early nineteenth century. I enjoyed carrying out and writing up the research part immensely, but sharing it in front of the whole group felt more like a nightmare than a dream come true. That part drove me stir crazy leading all the way up to it, as did the presentation itself, although the thought of doing it was definitely worse than the act, just about.

This was the way I had also experienced sharing in the class at primary and secondary school; there was always this fear that I'd stumble over my words, make a mistake and get laughed at. These are fears that I'm sure weren't at all helped by having hyper-critical parents who didn't know how to positively praise or encourage, either.

Even though my father did take an interest in my education, his methods of helping me keep up my grades left much to be desired. He focused solely on mistakes, and how stupid one had to be to have made them. On the other hand, in regard to education, my mum just left me to it. I think she expected me to do well in school because, from the offset, I seemed to be a bit more studious, especially compared to the rest of my siblings.

So, groups, and the expression of myself truly within them, let alone believing that I had something of importance to say, was a first for me. I was certain that other people would similarly think of me as stupid, and that I would literally shrivel up and die from feelings of absolute inadequacy, but I swallowed the fear, and despite being terrified, got on with it anyway. In fact, not only did I get on with it, what I researched, wrote and had to say was very well-liked and received, all of which made me ever so happy. It was a sweet victory!

The tutors felt that I had covered the subject very well, and that the critical analysis was clear, concise and valid. To cut a long story short, the whole college experience helped some way towards me becoming a more self-confident person, and also helped me to see, believe and appreciate that I do have intelligence, as well as worthwhile contributions to make. I truly enjoyed the total experience, in spite of my fears.

Generally, it felt so good having college to look forward to; having it to go to, and just being there among my peers. I was so glad that I hadn't let my initial anxieties and fears deter me, because for the first time in a very long time – or perhaps for the first time altogether – I began to feel like I fitted somewhere. On top of that, I didn't even find the work to be over and above me, like I had first feared would be the case, discovering along the way that perhaps I did have what it takes to actually do a degree of sorts. My tutors' belief in me went a long way towards making me feel that I was totally on track, worthy of a second chance and that, for me now, there was no turning back.

The growing confidence I was feeling continued to spill over into my eating. There still remained the worry, the monitoring and the ensuring that I wasn't comfort eating in the same old ways, as the temptation to do so, especially as a coping mechanism, was ever-present and at times strong. I had totally stopped vomiting, and even gone so far as to give my weighing scales away. One morning, as I was routinely weighing myself, I thought, *I can't live my life by the scales. I can't use them to decide what kind of day I'm going to have!* So, I just gave them to a friend and never bought another set again, although I did continue to weigh myself here and there at times while I was out and spotted some scales close by.

Also, by the following year I had stopped counting calories all together. Counting calories was a thing I had been doing religiously and automatically after eating, as well as overall at the end of the day, ever since my early teens when I first got caught up in the self-image, self-loathing, binge eating and dieting cycle. It was a challenge to stop counting calories initially, because it had given me a certain sense of reassurance and peace, especially when I'd had a 'good day' without overeating, among other things. If I had overeaten, then I could make what I felt were the necessary adjustments, namely eating fewer calories and just carrying on and forgiving myself. I was on a roll and good to go, so on the whole I felt confident enough to let counting calories go.

However, and without fully realising it, as the relationship with Ronald had come to a definite end, and I was making good progress in my relationship with food, I was developing another problem relationship, this time with cannabis. At the time, I didn't really see it as a problem. Smoking weed had been very much part of peer and family culture; it was an everyday reality. I suppose on a deeper level, similar to food, it was another way of attempting to fill up an inner emptiness; of filling up without needing, or having to depend on, unreliable people. Also, smoking cannabis gave me the illusion of having something to look forward to at the end of the day: of having something waiting at home for me.

Individual therapy sessions had started in October of 1987, around the same time as the course, which cushioned things and gave me the support that had been needed. Not that I ever used the therapy to talk about my weed smoking, or to analyse or understand the reasons behind it, mainly because at that time, like I said, I didn't see it as a problem. Also, it didn't seem like the right thing to do, since it seemed an anti-establishment act; anti-British culture and against the law. As such, I feared that I would be doubly judged, being perhaps already seen as mad, bad and black.

This particular bout of therapy was to last two years, and it further developed and expanded on some of the issues that had come up and out of the previous group experience, namely the emotional abuse, abandonment and eating disorder resolution themes, as well as the present day difficulties I was experiencing at the time, not withstanding, and in particular, the end of the relationship with Ronald. The sexual abuse never came up, for whatever reason.

In relation to the Ronald situation, we spent a lot of time exploring the ways in which him having a daughter had impacted me. It was like her presence had taken something important from me; I felt replaced, which was an experience I had already been familiar with, having oftentimes felt replaced and misplaced in my mother's affections.

As a young girl, I grew up feeling not good enough and unworthy of my mother's love because I didn't have long hair, unlike my sisters, especially Lauren; Lauren, my successor, who seemed to have it all: long hair, good looks and fairer skin. As a child, I never felt like a proper little girl. Plus, I had wanted to be the first to give Ronald a girl; I had wanted to be special in that way. Just like my brother Darrel was deemed that special thing when he was born, as the long-awaited son.

So, when we explored this whole area, especially those feelings, more of which were buried underneath and therefore hidden, it gave me further and deepening self-understanding, not to mention much-welcomed emotional release. Therapy was good for this; I always left feeling more at peace, more able to see and having a much clearer perspective.

Another key issue we explored related to the good, capable and helpful little girl of past, whose face I still wore, and which permeated almost every area in my then relationships and life; the Great Mother role that I couldn't quite release myself from. It was so very much a part of who I thought I was that it had become my very reason for being. For instance, once while in a therapy session, I was relaying to the therapist an experience I had once shared with Sharon, the girl I'd met in college and became fast friends with.

We were both sixteen at the time, and were exploring the modelling world. We had recently had our pictures taken, which came out very well, and therefore had us thinking that perhaps we had potential. So, we had taken ourselves off to these auditions for an upcoming fashion show event.

After doing our thing and strutting our inexperienced stuff, it had come to the part where we'd find out if we had been successful or not. Naturally, we were both very nervous, but Sharon was much more nervous, anxious and seemingly vulnerable than me; something that I had always sensed keenly from the very beginning of our relationship. I always felt that she saw me as much more experienced and worldly. Indeed, while growing up, I generally felt this way in regard to my peers, which made fitting in and feeling a part of them, and things, really hard. At times, it was an impossible task. Psychologically, I felt separate; cordoned off.

Anyway, I remember experiencing a certain kind of relief when Sharon went for a walk or to the shops or something of that sort. As luck would have it, I had thought at the time, they gave me the results while she was gone: we hadn't been successful. It was quite a dejecting experience, but I was quick to put those feelings away someplace and come up with a less upsetting account of why we hadn't been chosen, to lessen the blow for Sharon, or so I'd thought. I told her something like they had had enough models for now, but that they said they would contact us sometime in the future when they were putting on more shows. This embellished feedback had easily reassured her.

When I was relaying the story to the therapist, trying to show her, albeit unconsciously, what a good, considerate person I generally was, she turned it around on me. She, and indeed therapy, had a way of doing that, which on the one hand can feel quite liberating, but on the other can feel quite shaming, irritating, embarrassing and humiliating, like being caught in a (little white, unconscious) lie with yourself and the world.

The underbelly of it, as she interpreted and shared with me, was that my reaction in the situation with Sharon wasn't entirely and purely selfless, and that perhaps it was as much a need for me to have behaved in that way; a need for me to equally, however indirectly, protect, calm and reassure myself; a way of trying to overcome my own feelings of disappointment and rejection, while maintaining a certain emotional distance and control.

So, very basically, what I believed I was doing 'for Sharon' was (perhaps, and more immediately and importantly) also something I was doing for myself, the only way I knew how to, giving to myself through giving to others; emotional reassurance, once removed.

Truth be told, I oftentimes felt lost in relationships; lost in the needs of others; lost and not quite sure where others began and I ended, or was it where I began and others ended? Is it just the same thing, whichever way around? When I helped 'others' it made me feel 'good.' Nothing wrong with that, but for the likes of me, that give and take in relationships was completely out of sync, and therefore not really good for me. Those second-hand 'good feelings' couldn't take away the bad ones that I often felt —and cordoned off-deep down inside.

The therapist's interpretations made me feel like I had been caught in a lie; caught in a 'hiding & denied place,' which the therapist herself was trying to find and have more direct contact with. The truth of her observations hurt, especially the overall experience of having someone seeming to look through you and know you better than you are knowing yourself. However, deep down in that feeling bad and completely let down secret hideaway place, those same observations and words continued to filter through and shed light.

The insight of my being way out of balance in regard to my giving and receiving in relationships helped me to see, and appreciate again, something core and fundamental about myself and my way of being and relating in the world. At that time, there were a lot of people who depended on me much more than I did them. One of those had been my sister Beverly, who I did a lot of babysitting for, looking after my nieces Tasha, then nine, and Sara, three.

Beverly had been going through a need to rave and see what her partner was up to phrase at that time. To me, it seemed like the kids and their needs were not being fully considered or sufficiently responded to. That resonated with me deeply, reminding me of how life had been for us as children, so there I went, attempting to meet those needs and fill that void. There was also another friend whose daughter I had also felt the need to rescue, and so there were often a number of children at my house, which I altogether didn't mind most of the time, especially with Jamie being an only child. I had felt that they also provided him company, as well as the opportunity to be a part of an extended family outside of just him and me.

In addition to minding kids, there was always a regular influx of adults seeking and needing support. However, even though at times, either consciously or unconsciously, I got something from it, it drove me crazy because it was such a constant. Almost every week I would be asked to babysit, which I would do because I found it hard to say no. It all got on my last nerve sometimes, especially because the 'demands' didn't seem to take into consideration my own needs and wants, especially my own need and want for support. It was all extremely one-sided and emotionally draining, but I continued to do it anyway, a thing that sometimes brought with it gnawing resentment, which I buried.

Another important issue that also began to get addressed in therapy was finances. There was a time when finances became a real strain again, so much so that I couldn't find the money to pay for the sessions, which cost about £7, and at those times I stayed away. I also used to stay away from sessions when I felt particularly depressed, feeling that I had to 'spare the therapist' from my depression and financial difficulties, just like I felt I had to keep my feelings and other problems to myself while growing up. To me, that was what was meant to be 'strong' and 'good' and 'grown up.'

In regard to finances, I really did believe that there wasn't any other way around the subject other than to quietly not turn up for sessions. It was like I couldn't imagine being given to without giving something directly back in return, and to discuss it seemed too embarrassing, even shameful, but discuss it we did. All issues got addressed, as there's no hiding place in therapy; no slipping away quietly out of the picture. In regard to the money I owed, the therapist waived that, as well as any future fees, until I could afford it. I couldn't believe it. I couldn't believe that she would make such a concession for me, rather than have me pay or leave.

Nor could I get my head around the fact that she *especially* wanted to see me when I was feeling bad- meaning low. I remember feeling so indebted, happy and grateful to her. The idea of someone being there for me without me having to repay them in some way, without faking 'togetherness,' 'strength' or 'happiness,' really did seem quite mind-boggling, yet totally reassuring on a level that was corner-turning. I was also enjoying the sessions, and so I didn't really want to stay away, or see it end just yet.

When the therapy finally did come to an end, I left it feeling that there was still more to be done, for even though I had gained a lot, like with the group therapy before, I still felt the need for more. It still very much felt 'tip of the iceberg,' and like I hadn't had my fill yet. As a result, it took a while to come to terms with the end of this bout of therapy. I missed it terribly to begin with.

During that time, I began to write creatively about my experiences of 'being' thus far, more as a way of coming to terms with the ending of therapy, while also integrating the insights it had given me, into something new and available. It was like the therapist had left me with the baby me that had once been left to care for itself way too early, and way before it really knew what it was doing. Now, however, it was my adult self's responsibility.

It took some getting used to, knowing what to do and how to respond to my own feelings and needs. I tried to manage it as best I could, which left much room for improvement, as I was smoking more dependently at the time as a way of managing, coping and numbing those very difficult, vulnerable, painfully lonely and sad feelings. At the same time, there I was juggling single parenthood with academic life, after I had successfully completed the access course and secured a place at the then Polytechnic of East London.

I had started university in October 1988, so by the time the therapy sessions ended, I had completed year one and was due to start year two. I had gotten onto a multi-subject, three-year degree course. The first year had been fairly challenging, but a challenge I was still happy to take on, even though a more insecure part of me continued to wander if doing a degree was indeed out of my reach. I took it one step at a time and stuck with it, though. Plus, I was in love with the library; more stuff to read and more lessons to learn! One of my favourites was Erich Fromm.

At the end of the first year, I obtained a good 57% grade, but the perfectionist in me was determined to get an even better mark in the years that followed. With the encouragement of one of the course tutors, who went on to become my personal tutor, and was generally a great source of help and support to me throughout, I switched course when I returned for the second year in 1989. I moved onto a single-honours Psycho-Social degree course with professional studies. I joined it in the second year, so had three years remaining.

The course was heavily based on psychoanalysis, which allowed for the experience and consideration of leaning towards a career in psychodynamic counselling, as well as social services-type work, and having experienced the wonders that therapy could bring, I had already been considering that kind of employment.

I truly enjoyed the course, even though it was very challenging in places, and I was glad that I had made the switch. The challenge mainly came from the demands made by combining studying with single parenthood, and especially in the way of the financial considerations and constraints that studying placed upon me. But once started, I wanted to prove to myself that I could do it; that with hard work and pure determination, I could succeed, and succeed I did. I truly surprised myself!

In the ensuing three years, I ended up doing extremely well, particularly in exams. This was an area where I'd feared that I would have done worst of all, but it ended up being quite the reverse. So, steadily, certainly and annually, my work and grades got better and better, culminating with me leaving the course in 1992 with a 65% upper-second honours degree, and even receiving a 62% for my 15,000-word dissertation, which I wrote on 'people's experiences of psychotherapy; what helps and hinders positive outcomes.' I was so pleased and proud of myself. I had really worked my butt off for it.

I had also done exceptionally well in the counselling aspect of the degree course, gaining an 89% in the final year exam. The course had been heavily psychoanalytically-based, in line with the passion and expertise of my very patient, understanding, kind and supportive personal tutor, on whom I must admit to having had quite bit of a crush. He was also, to my mind, an excellent teacher and very thoughtful. I used to love the free, easy and informative way that he delivered his lectures.

Outside of university, I used to accompany him to various discourse lectures on themes and perspectives in psychoanalytical thought, an experience I enjoyed immensely. All of these things made me that much more convinced in regard to my vocational aspirations, and subsequently, in order to gain further experience, I applied to, and later became, a volunteer counsellor at Mind in Haringey. This was a position I took up in August 1992, after completing the psychosocial studies degree course.

After the course had finished, I'd contemplated doing a master's degree on the subject of Eating Disorders, but then decided to instead build up my professional expertise and experience, as well as my bank balance. However, during the summer, and outside of the volunteer work at Mind, I also took the time to recharge my batteries, enjoy some 'free time' and chill out with my son, who was nine years old by then.

As much as I'd enjoyed the course, it was such a relief to be free of all the studying, revising, worrying and juggling that had been my lot for five very long years. However, applying for and getting onto, that access course remains one of the best moves I have ever made.

In regard to the desire, during the academic experience, to have built up a better network of friends, sadly this was not to be. Socialising had always been difficult; it was enough dividing study time and giving myself and Jamie individual time without worrying if I was taking something crucial away from him; something important that he should be getting. I was still keen to give him the best start possible; the one I never had. Financial constraints also kept certain things and activities very much in place and, it seemed, way out of reach.

I did make some there and then new friends, though; I was good at that. Not so much in an overt, intentional way, but more of an accidental, by the by kind of way. I kept running hard into the unconscious pattern of others seeming to *need* more from me, which (once again) automatically saw me falling into the role of 'all-giving, understanding great mother mummy.'

I still did not know how to properly be, or indeed if I should even allow myself to be, on the receiving end in relationships. It was like this with one female friend who I did kind of get close to on the course, and she to me. However, towards the end of the course, her neediness and my own inability to set boundaries and share my own vulnerabilities began to weigh heavily on me, so I let the relationship go. That was a bit sad really, because looking back, if I – if we – had known how to save it, I believe we would have still been friends to this very day, as we had overall got on really well, and had shared together a great sense of humour.

Overall, returning to higher education and doing exceptionally well made me feel, on some level, that I had put to right a wrong. The wrong was not being given the opportunity to do well enough in school; not as well as I knew I could have done if I hadn't been left so totally to my own devices; if I had been given better and wiser counsel, and my childhood hadn't been so terribly wanting.

As a child, in and out of school, I was too preoccupied to learn. I was preoccupied with things that a child should not have to be concerned with in a so-called civilised society, like what I would eat so as not to feel so hungry all the time, how I would occupy my time so not to feel so bored, alone and overwhelmed all the time, and how I would keep myself safe and away from harm.

BOOK TWO:

INSIDE-OUT

CHAPTER TWO

In regard to intimacy, I had been single and celibate during my years at university, from spring 1990 to the spring of '93. It wasn't that I set out to be celibate, it just came about after a spell of disappointing relationships post-Ronald. Let me go back a little. Four months after Ronald and I (finally) broke up in the spring of 1988, I had a fleeting attempt at a relationship with a guy called Simon. He was one of the many guys who I knew from the raving scene, who I was faintly aware liked me. He was aware that Ronald and I had broken up, so didn't delay in making a move, whereupon I responded by inviting him to my house the following Friday evening.

The evening went well, and I was surprised to find myself warming to him. We just talked, listened to music and shared a joint, and that was that. We also kept in touch during the week by phone. During the following meeting at my house, he made his feelings known, saying how much he liked me and for how long this had been the case, and how he desired to be with me, especially physically.

I remember feeling both excited and nervous after his declaration of feelings – feelings that remained all week and left me with essentially warm and desirable feelings towards him also, and hope-filled daydreams of love having perhaps found me at last. It had felt so good to be desired and to be wanted by a man again; to be, I guess, in good, healthy libido. I had thought and feared that, after Ronald, letting myself have feelings for another man would be near impossible, so these feelings towards Simon seemed positive and reassuring.

Sadly, though, by the time we got to our next date, things turned sour when he decided to tell me then that he was already seeing someone else; the mother of his children. From where I was standing, it became painfully clear to me that he was just after a certain kind of relationship with me as a 'bit on the side,' rather than anything meaningful or significant. So, I ended it, as whatever it was, it wasn't for me. I had already been there and done that. It didn't seem right just having sex for the sake of it, especially with someone already spoken for, even though I was tempted. I wanted much more; something more solid, real and lasting. Even after Ronald, I still held onto 'the dream.'

Needless to say, I was somewhat disappointed and pissed. I was mainly angry because it felt like he had strung me along by not telling me from the outset that he was otherwise engaged. For me, when a family is involved (meaning children), there is no way I could go there; that seemed too wrong. Still, it was good to know that there was indeed life after Ronald, and that the experience of him hadn't killed such feelings and desires off completely

Michael Davidson came along a little while later, during that summer of 1988. He had heard from my sister Lauren that Ronald and I had broken up, and she encouraged him to make contact with me, suggesting that I could do with some cheering up. However, Michael and I already had history. At the age of fifteen, sixteen, he had been my first real boyfriend.

Ronald had been my first true, obsessive love, in the sense of a 'women who love too much.' On the other hand, Michael was my first romance; my first true 'poppy love.' I met Michael at our school disco, where Lauren had introduced us. He was tall, dark and, I thought, handsome, in a 'rebel without a cause,' broody kind of way. When he made his advances towards me that night, I felt truly bowled over. I felt this way because he was older than me – four years, to be exact – so was more experienced and from the in crowd. I found his whole demeanour extremely intriguing, appealing and captivating. Plus, you could tell that he loved music, and he moved well. When we danced together that just sealed things: it was like *magic*. He had smelled so good, as well!

I also looked really good myself that night. I wore a black with silver trimmings gypsy top that fell at the shoulders, a flowing black and silver skirt and headscarf wrapped in style, along with black sling-back shoes. My mum had lent those items to me; she had a great wardrobe, one to die for. She had also put makeup on me that night; she was very good at applying it, and used to do all her friends' whenever they were going out. She was very creative and expressive in that way.

Anyway, after applying my makeup, she looked at me. She

really looked at me and, I believed, saw me for the very first time. She saw my beauty, and said out loud in astonishment, *Marcia is really quite pretty, you know*. It was like she never knew this before; she hadn't taken the time to see this about me.

That falling in love night, my mother saw the same beauty that I used to spend ages in the mirror looking for as a child. It's like even though a part of me believed I was ugly, another part, some unknown part buried deep down inside, knew this just wasn't the case; knew that even with short hair I was inside-out beautiful. Anyway, that evening, her doing my makeup and the longed-for 'true-self' acknowledgment had felt like coming home. It made me believe, in that precious moment of time, that finally, in her eyes, I was indeed special, unique, and a sight to behold.

That unexpected interaction with my mother played a part in the magical meeting with Michael. He and I had a great time, and the disco was slamming as well. All my friends were there from school, the raving scene and the youth centre that I used to go. Even the teachers loosened up that night, letting their hair down and their dancing feet do what they wanted, though I couldn't identify the exact tune that they were dancing to, which gave us jokes all night long. Still, I loved the way that in spite of their lack of rhythm, they just didn't care; they just kept jigging away to the music regardless. I admire people who can dance and live so freely, and to their own tune.

The night, especially dancing arms in arms with Michael, was all very romantic. I really did fall in love with him, Mills & Boon paperback-style, and needless to say, we started dating not too long afterwards. We spent a lot of time together. He had his own music system and a great record collection, and when we listened to music together, I would feel comfortable enough around him to sing; the only man to that date I'd felt comfortable singing in front of. Michael really did have a sweet, sensitive, caring and charming side to him, so much so that at the beginning of our courtship, those qualities made it really easy to be with him; to relate to him and to love him.

Not too long after we'd started to go out, my mum left for the States, but before leaving she had encouraged me to go on the pill. She never prohibited Michael from spending the night, even though for me it was difficult at first. My mother always maintained that she would rather her daughter's boyfriends stay at the family home rather than have her girls feel that they had to sleep out to be with their boyfriends. In her eyes, teenagers would be teenagers, and she'd rather have her girls 'being teenagers' under her roof, so at night she knew exactly where they were.

She was quite relaxed, liberal, and broad-minded in that regard, as well as completely untraditional in some of her views, which made us the envy of most our friends, and her a bit perverse in the eyes of their parents. At that time, and in a lot of ways, I actually loved this about my mother- her 'liberal, matter of fact and couldn't-care-less-what-others thought' ways.

In regard to the contraceptive pill, it was really interesting going to get it from the local family planning clinic. It was like they found it hard to believe that at my age, my mother had given me permission to be on the pill; I think they thought that I was making it up. At one point, it seemed as if they were still going to deny me it, even though I was sixteen years old and had had my mother's permission, but I was adamant that I would have it, one way or another, which I did after some to-ing and fro-ing.

It was Michael who had introduced me to marijuana. Well, not exactly, since weed smoking and selling had already been a regular feature of my everyday childhood life, on both my mother and father's sides. My mother didn't sell weed, she just smoked it and was associated with others who sold and smoked it. But Michael was the first boyfriend who had smoked it, and he had taught me how to roll it for him, which I quite enjoyed doing, even though I was never tempted to smoke myself, and he never encouraged it.

Michael and I lasted about five- six months, whereupon I went from him straight into the arms of Ronald. I had wanted to leave Michael a couple of months before, as he had become increasingly unpredictable, moody, jealous and controlling. On a number of occasions when we were out, he would turn up and insist I go home. He even used to forbid me from going out or wearing shorts, even though it was the summertime.

That had been the story of Michael and me, but over the years I knew that he still continued to carry a torch for me. I remember him visiting me at my sister Beverly's house, bringing flowers and a card not too long after I came home from the hospital with Jamie. I had thought that it was so sweet, as well as very big of him. So, when he turned up at my house in 1988, seven years later, needless to say I was very surprised. I was further surprised when, after a little while, I fell in love with him all over again. Letting myself fall for him actually helped me to finally let go of the relationship with Ronald. I remember that being the exact time that Ronald and I truly became history in my mind...

Michael had not too long re-entered the scene, and I wasn't quite sure whether or not I wanted to have anything to do with him, but then one evening, out of sheer boredom and mischievousness, and I guess loneliness, I called Susan's number again. To my utter surprise, Ronald had answered, whereupon I had flung the phone down, once again feeling hurt and betrayed, even though by that time things between us had been over for at least five months. It was after this incident that I had said to myself that I might as well get on with my life, as Ronald was clearly getting on with his.

This time around, Michael wasn't at all controlling and domineering. I didn't even think on that anyway – I wasn't worried about it; he just became for me a pleasant distraction. However, I did go on to develop quite strong feelings for him, mainly because, as a person, he was a lot more attentive, touchy, feely and emotionally available than Ronald ever was, and in a way that didn't always have to lead to sex. I had been so starved and deprived of this kind of intimacy and touch that I lapped it all up.

Michael and I used to go out clubbing every Friday night and have ourselves such a great time. I loved spending time with him, especially dancing with him; there was such chemistry between us. When we danced, it felt nothing less than divine, and always like the (very) first time. It was still all so very romantic.

Unfortunately, it soon came to pass that I was not the only woman in Michael's life. He shared this information with me a couple of months into the relationship. He was living with someone who he expressed feeling a certain and definite obligation towards, her having stood by him through some troubled times. I was able to get all this information from him when I noticed that in between and after our great together times, he would regularly disappear, literally without word, for three, four or five days. At the time, I couldn't understand why he would or could disappear like that, because our times together always left me wanting more. I began to wonder why he wasn't feeling the exact same way. It just didn't make sense.

The situation with Michael and his girlfriend brought me lots of pain. Once again, it seemed I was being denied the very thing I wanted most. So, I hanged on in there for another three months or so, thinking that somehow what we had and felt for each other would see us through. I even suggested, a month or so later, after he had first hinted at it to me himself, that he move in with me, but he declined. For whatever reason, he seemed to have had a change of heart, which had made me feel painfully rejected.

In the end, it was the regular and consistent pattern of us spending really good quality time together, and then him disappearing for days, and later a couple of weeks, at a time, which brought the greatest pain and saw me crying my heart out without end, night after night. It was like some great big wound had been reopened, like I was crying all at once for everything that had thus far happened to me and had been denied me, relationship-wise. It was like I was truly grieving the break up between Ronald and I for the first time. Whatever it was, I didn't quite understand at the time why I was crying so much, and on a daily basis.

I didn't bring this situation into therapy much at the time. I didn't feel that I could tell the therapist the whole story, and besides, I felt embarrassed, ashamed and a fool. However, in spite of it all, I felt sorry for Michael. I could see how pressured, overwhelmed and confused he was, and to top it all off, he was a chronic people pleaser; he desperately tried to please and meet everybody's needs, all at the same time! All of that made the anger I felt towards him become somewhat impotent, to be replaced with a familial pity and later compassion, especially after we had an open and frank conversation about his situation.

He shared with me that although he loved me and wanted to be with me, he felt that I was too good for him. I heard him out, and it was at that point I realised it was all about him, and we couldn't work anyway because he truly didn't believe that he deserved me...

The openness and honesty of the admission had left me, in spite of everything, with some kind of respect still intact for him. Luckily, at the time I had therapy for support, and I had my studies and my darling, precious son Jamie to keep me focused and keeping on. So, when I stopped crying, when it was truly over, I refocused and got busy again.

Around the same time, 1990-91, the relationship with my mother, and to a certain extent a few of my siblings and old school friends, remained strained. I had changed and still was very much changing and growing, and had picked up on the fact that people found this hard to deal with. They found it hard to relate to my being in higher education and all that they thought it entailed, all of which seemed to set me further apart from them.

In regard to my mum in particular, she still wasn't open to discussing the past, let alone acknowledge its continued after-effects. She also found it difficult to accept the fact that I had a mind of my own, and that I was coming into myself and therefore letting go of the role of being her good, compliant little girl.

I was very much separating from her, and I sensed that she felt threatened by this, but at the same time, because I was the only one in the family who had ever made this kind of change, it made it easier for her and a few of siblings to view the resultant unease and conflicts as solely a 'Marcia problem.' After all, hadn't Marcia always been 'different?'

During this time that I decided to lock my hair; one day I just had the thought that no matter high up the ladder I got, I would never want to sacrifice or compromise my cultural and racial identity. Whatever group I was going to end up being a part of in the future, I still wanted to be proud and feel very much involved in my African and Caribbean heritage. Basically, I wasn't going to 'sell out' in order to fit in anywhere I may later find myself. Besides, I had stopped perming my hair because it was ruining it, a thing I clearly began to notice after having gone through a six-month period of just plaiting it, whereupon it really picked up, which further suggested to me that my hair generally does better left to its own devices, as near to natural as possible.

It was quite an experience deciding to lock my hair; it was and has been a journey in and of itself. I got a lot of anxious and negative comments from some family members and friends with their main concerns being, *What if you change your mind and no longer wanted it locked? What if it doesn't look good? What will people say/*

think? What if it stops you from getting ahead? However, I persisted on, because deep down inside I knew it was the right thing for me, that I wouldn't be changing my mind for now, and that nothing could stop me from being and becoming who or what I pleased.

I still have locks now, and they have never stopped or hindered me in any way. My locks went on to grow very long, and many times over, as I had cut them in length here and there over the years. They grew much more than I had ever dreamed my hair could; much more than I would have ever believed if someone had told me as a child, *Don't worry, your hair, like Rapunzel's, will grow.*

Perhaps the fairies truly did hear all my wishes, back when I was a child blowing on many a dandelion, believing the seed heads were indeed fluffy fairies themselves, who I would ask to let my hair grow long enough so that I could, at the very least, get it cornrowed like everybody else, and get to look and feel like a real life little girl; so, having my hair grow as an adult like that, way down into my back, felt like nothing short of a miracle.

BOOK TWO:

INSIDE-OUT

CHAPTER THREE

Due to the disappointing relationships I kept experiencing with men, I decided that I would never again enter another relationship lightly. During this the time of singledom, I was focused, as usual, on my studies, being a good parent and further understanding and developing my true self and the full range of its expression. I also decided to put myself back into therapy in order to continue to dismantle the isolation and loneliness that still plagued me, and to also get to whatever was still at the bottom of things. These sessions began in March 1991.

I met my new therapist through the Inner-City Centre, via, once again, the Women's Therapy Centre. The sessions took place at an organisation called AGIP (Association of Group and Individual Psychotherapy), and they were, initially, weekly and open-ended, which basically meant that treatment would go on for as long as I felt the need for it. This was a welcome change that came as a real relief, as both previous experiences of therapy had only lasted for a set period of time.

Being single at the time helped me to focus more on myself, and in a sense helped me to go even deeper into the healing process. I was determined that there would be no hiding place in this particular bout of therapy, and at the time, because of all that I had been through recently, I absolutely didn't want there to be. It felt like I still had loads to (un) learn.

My experiences with my new therapist, Caroline, came to be a rich and meaningful experience, and somewhere deep inside, I truly did come to view her as 'mother figure.' There was no denying the transference process, meaning the way in which I brought into the therapeutic situation, and indeed in varying degrees to all of life's situations and relationships, old hopes, fears, tattered dreams and patterned ways of being and relating. It just all spontaneously happens outside of immediate awareness.

This thought is very scary to some, the unconscious at work, as oftentimes we prefer to hold onto the myth of our having *total* control of ourselves and all of our facilities, and I was no different. However, when we trust in the process of being open and honest, it makes for an awesome and miraculous process, engagement and self-transformation; one that always makes life that bit more interesting and worth the living and exploration.

In my therapeutic encounters with Caroline, I experienced myself a lot of the time as a little girl trying to be and appear grown up, which made the experience of building up trust with her difficult. Perhaps even more difficult was the building of trust with my very own mother, a building that never quite got started, let alone completed, and was a very painful, uncertain and unpredictable experience. So, the much-needed building of trust in the therapeutic relationship with Caroline brought with it many archaic unresolved conflicts, as well as painful and uncomfortable feelings of neediness – a neediness and dependency I tend to want to flee from.

There was also this all-encompassing sense of shame that took up residence throughout the whole experience. Even at the best of times, I used to find it really hard to meet Caroline's gaze in dialogue during sessions. I remember feeling compelled to bow my head in an unconscious shame, and I could only just about maintain eye contact when it was my turn to talk. I was always expecting to be judged, scolded and rejected, like had been the way of things for me as a child. I felt so little and terribly flawed in the meeting of her gaze, so unworthy of her care, so it felt less emotionally painful to bow my head.

I also had this immense, yet undefined and unfathomable, fear that I would overburden Caroline and inadvertently damage or cause her way too much stress and pain with my neediness. Along with all these fears and concerns was this intense need for her acceptance and approval, as well as the need to be her 'good little girl.' To me, being Caroline's 'good little girl' meant doing exactly what was expected of me by causing her very little trouble and wanting for nothing.

All these things I felt most keenly and uncomfortably, both consciously and unconsciously, being in the world of self-recovery. The process felt like being under local anaesthetic, where you get to both have the experience of feeling and not feeling what is going on at the same time.

Holidays were also painful for me, as they brought to the surface, unconsciously at first, very disturbing and painful feelings of rejection and abandonment – the kind I used to feel and experience as a child, especially during my mother's departures – which Caroline eased by giving me permission to own those difficult feelings and put them into words.

To begin with, I did find Caroline's insistence upon looking at, understanding and acknowledging these hidden unconscious feelings a bit out of place, as well as a bit of a nuisance. However, in time I came to see just how far removed I had come to be from my inner world of thoughts and most true and troubled feelings. I came to see how I had pushed certain memories and feelings out, and how difficult it now was for me to be letting them back in properly, from the front, not the back, door.

Caroline allowed me to express my anger, helping me to see the justification in it and behind it. She was my 'It's OK to be angry' therapist, and it was totally a new experience being so directly encouraged to own and feel my feelings, especially feelings of anger. Anger was a feeling, which as a good little girl, I'd had major difficulty with. There was much to be very angry about as a child, but I grew up conditioned to believe that I wasn't entitled to it. In fact, not only was I not entitled to be angry, I should have been most grateful of all that was done for me; turning my anger into guilt…

It took some work and energy, facing and feeling the depth of my feelings, as well as dealing with my vulnerabilities and learning to trust Caroline. Still, as difficult as it was, it was also very liberating; a most welcomed relief. As I've already mentioned, I kept confusing Caroline with my mother and earlier life experiences, which was mainly the transference at work, because that's how therapy and healing works. In the ambiguity of the transference situation, I continued to wrestle with reconciling who I was becoming with the unmet needs of the 'good little girl' who just wanted to do what was expected and gain approval. That was what she was familiar with, not with allowing the transformative power of anger.

Caroline wouldn't let me be the little girl who just puts up and shuts up and did what was expected. Time after time, she would turn my attention to what was really going on; to what I was unconsciously acting out, encouraging me to reclaim what was truly bothering me in any given moment. She allowed me to be mad at her if that was how I felt, which seemed and felt so wrong to me, but Caroline wouldn't have it any other way, which I really grew to love about her. She was so open, honest, direct, caring and genuine; a real solid presence, then and throughout.

During that time, similar to how I previously likened the experience of therapy to being under local anaesthetic, it was like I was living in two worlds: the past and the present. In the present, I had Jamie and my studies to ground me. I also had weed to calm and comfort me, or so I thought that's what it was doing. I couldn't really afford the weed, though, but I'd unwittingly grown quite psychologically dependent on it by then.

Mixed in with the dependency that was taking root was an ever-increasing desire to be free of it, especially once I became aware that it was now adding to my stress rather than alleviating it. This hoped-for stress reliever was instead creating an inner divide in me, as I argued with myself for and against its use. Like a relationship gone bad, cannabis no longer kept its promises; no longer gave me what I needed, if it ever really had.

Smoking weed was becoming quite a disappointing habit, and one that I felt unable to quit, but at that time it didn't feel like a pressing issue to have fixed within the confines of therapy. Instead, I essentially used therapy to get to the root of other equally important or underlying problems, especially the understanding of my anger and rage; the storing of which I had kept secluded underground, under lock and key. It wasn't only the anger, but also the realisation of the depth of other deprivations, like the lack of food while growing up, and how hungry I got and felt at times.

It often felt like I was left waiting for the next meal, the next day, or the next time somebody passed a little change my way and I could get my beloved, self-soothing sweets. When my mother was away this hungering experience intensified as I did not want to make any kind of demands on the numerous substitute care-givers I stayed with.

I also shared with Caroline my regular Saturday afternoons pastime of begging on the streets for money, not only to buy sweets, but also, and especially, to buy dolls and doll's clothes at Zodiac toy store in Stoke Newington. I loved my dolls, and being in that toyshop, and being able to buy something, made me super happy. Being a proactive person, taking the bull by the horns in my life at that time gave my days purpose and meaning. It made me feel hopeful that I could try and make things better for myself. It kept me keeping on.

Dolls were my life, and I treated them as if they were really alive. They gave me many years of much-needed fulfilment, and I sought and played with them right up until I was thirteen, whereupon they began to lose their flavour. This change had felt quite sad, like a loss, as my dolls had previously occupied so much of my time and had been a much-needed distraction from the overwhelming feelings of abandonment.

When the desire for dolls began to dissipate, it had put me back into more direct contact with an inner, utter emptiness. I believe that was one of the reasons why, not too long afterward, I turned to food. An eating disorder swiftly developed and took up equal amounts of much-needed distraction time, totally engaging me body, soul and especially mind.

Hand in hand with the deprivation, Caroline and I spent a good amount of time looking at and acknowledging how affected I had been by my mother's constant comings and goings, and how I had come to feel responsible for her running off and away like that, and abandoning us. It was as if we had overburdened her and ruined her life in some way, which was why she needed her space; why she had to get away, and also why she yelled and cursed at us when she was emotionally overwhelmed with her lot.

I'd taken all of these words to heart and swallowed them up. I'd believed my mother, hence my inability to lean on and allowing myself to be properly supported by people, or to willingly sharing my vulnerabilities and fears and expecting them to be sufficiently met. When I did manage to do this, like I was doing with Caroline, it was hard for me not feel that I 'owed' her something in return for being there and giving and caring about me and my well-being like that.

All of this I endeavoured to air and share with Caroline, even though it felt wrong doing so, as if I was betraying and selling my mother out; like I was being a very bad little girl, going against the grain. At the same time, though, I needed someone like Caroline to know how it was for me, and to have her share her understanding. The more of her understanding she gave, as well as her acceptance, support and indeed love, the more the need became to continue the unburdening. So, for what seemed like the first time in my life, I was having a real, deep, open and honest relationship with someone other than myself, even if I had to pay for it, which at the time only cost me £5 per session.

Throughout our time together, I did occasionally try and 'equalise' the relationship, because it had felt ever so uncomfortable and totally unfamiliar being solely on the receiving end of good nourishment. I had tried to do this more unconsciously than anything else, which Caroline lovingly brought to my attention. I did it by trying to engage with her more 'intellectually,' appearing instead to be a clever little big girl, rather than the emotional needy blob of a mess that I mostly and secretly felt. Plus, there was the depth of gratitude I felt towards her for essentially showing that she cared, and being so totally reliable and consistent with it. I wanted her to realise the immense gratitude I felt for her actually *hearing* all I had to say and responding in kind, allowing me to be my total self, warts and all.

Three months into the therapy, Caroline noticed how challenging the process was for me due to the depth of growth and change I was undertaking, and suggested that I think about coming to see her twice a week. At first, I thought, *She thinks I'm getting worse instead of better – that I'm not coping!* Horror of horrors! This made me feel insecure and deeply flawed, but after discussing it further with her, and sorting out what I could realistically afford to pay, which was £15-a-week for two sessions – a bargain – I thought, *What the heck, it couldn't hurt.*

Later on, when I was experiencing financial woes, the fee was reduced to just £10, which brought up difficult feelings again for me, the main one being that here I was again, taking without truly giving, a side of the fence that I so wasn't used to occupying. It's like I couldn't believe that people could want what's best for me, simply because they thought I deserved it; simply because they liked me and because they cared.

That people could truly want to help me without trying to help themselves seemed unbelievable to me, when the reality is that's how human beings are supposed to act and be with each other. These are the essential qualities that are supposed to set us apart from the so-called animals, but I was not at all used to experiencing them.

Not too long after I started therapy, and he had heard about it, the family friend who had sexually abused me as a child began visiting me; most regularly and urgently, I had noticed. He even took to turning up when I was due to have a therapy session, going so far as to accompany me to the doorstep of sessions on a couple of occasions.

Soon enough, and rather guiltily, he also brought up his sexual abuse of me; trying to justify it, and to alleviate his unconscious guilt and shame by making excuses for it. Excuses like, he had felt sorry for me, especially the way my mother used to treat me, whereupon I had indignantly and in disbelief replied, 'So that's what you do when you feel sorry for children – you fucking sexually abuse them?!'

In other conversations that followed, I deduced that he was implying that he also sexually abused me to get back at my mother for some misfortune she had caused him. In the mix of it, he tried to blow me off track by insinuating that my father was gay, and bringing up some kind of disturbing situation that my brother Darrel apparently witnessed as a child, although he wouldn't come out and plainly say what that something was. As it went on, it was like he wanted to find out, without asking, exactly how much of 'the past' I had remembered and shared in therapy. He was perhaps also thinking that if he disclosed and admitted to what he done to me, it would deter me from going any further with it, at least during therapy. He was real nervous.

At that time, I both was and wasn't totally in touch with the full extent of my anger, whether generally or towards him specifically. My childhood had left me very numb in places, and I still felt, deep down, that I deserved the things that had happened to me, so had no right to feel and be angry about them. Therapy was still the only place I could just about feel and be with anger. Also, anger had been very much out of control during my childhood, both on my mother and father's side. As a child, I had witnessed many instances of violence, some of which I was the direct victim of.

Before too long, and within the confines of therapy, the suppression of my anger began to rise further. Caroline encouraged it, never missing the opportunity to remind me that the anger was a healthy and natural response to all that had happened to me. She felt that not acknowledging and dealing with anger directly gets in the way of a more robust and complete (as complete as complete can be) recovery. She had likened it to having an operation that would most assuredly make one's prognosis for recovery from a potentially life-threatening condition much more of a guarantee than if the person went without.

When she had put it like that, I knew exactly what she meant and thus began to make much more of a concerted effort to allow angry feelings to flow, and I began to tentatively stand, face-to-face with the particular experiences that had built up inside this unacknowledged storehouse of anger. Deep down, I was still filled with the fears of what ifs: *What if my anger got out of control? What if my anger killed someone? What if it killed me? Where would expressing and engaging my anger lead?*

However, as time went on, the only thing my anger killed was the old me, the false me and the only person I'd felt able to be; the only part of me deemed likeable and acceptable to others. Relinquishing this self-denying side was very hard. In places, it felt like total self-annihilation and an actual physical passing, which was scary and confusing at times, like I was deliberately hurting rather than helping myself.

As I began to come more into my own, discovering my true identity, the situation with the abuser came to a head and led to the decision to confront him face-to-face on behalf of my true self and the unconscious anger and rage his actions had left in its wake. I had told Caroline about his sexual abuse, and had also shared with her the growing desire I had been feeling to confront him, especially in the light of his current, constant sabotaging contacts. She replied that she would support me in whatever I decided to do, but she felt that before I acted we should look more into the confrontation situation and explore all of its potential unfolding dynamics, as this would better prepare and equip me.

To a certain extent, we were able to do this here and there, in between the other day-to-day issues presented in any given session. What made me finally decide to act more spontaneously and intuitively– what gave me the energy and courage – was a dream I had that very same week. The dream was about the first time the abuser had sexually abused me, or at least the first time it happened at his house. In the dream, I had been fully aware of how it, and how it had felt, and the way it had impacted me. I had re-experienced the full range of my past and present feelings; the fear, the shock, the disbelief, the confusion, the dawning betrayal, the shame, the rage of feeling and being so wronged. Unlike how I had previously been conditioned to be, just taking and putting up with it, I was abso-fucking-lutely angry.

I was letting him have it, cursing him out, screaming and shouting. I was like a woman possessed, and it wasn't only him I was angry with in the dream, but also my mum. In the dream, she was an *ineffectual bystander*, just looking on, and then off- rooted to the stop-in another direction. She seemed to have no purpose; she was just standing there, of little use to me, a part of the furniture if you like, doing absolutely nothing to help or prevent what was going on. So, I confronted him a couple of days later at my house. I had written him a letter, which I read out. The letter went into my deep and true feelings of how it had been for me being sexually abused by him, and how it had affected my life. All of my feelings and being went into that letter.

He listened until I had finished, and then automatically, and obviously guiltily, went totally on the defensive, offering up his well-rehearsed and usual denials and excuses designed to justify and absolve him of responsibility. He denied sexually abusing me at the age I stated, saying that it must have been someone else, which at that time made a part of me begin to wonder if I had gotten it (all) wrong; that maybe he was right and perhaps there had been someone else, which later on, and in hindsight, I guessed was his manipulative intention, to confuse and throw me off track...

Perhaps he felt he could make me doubt my own memory if he'd noticed that I had not fully remembered the correct timing of when the molestation started. Like I mentioned before, I think he started molesting me even earlier, but being as young as I was, the exact timing of the memory is difficult to pin down.

It is so horribly frustrating to not remember events exactly as they happened, and when trying to put the shattered psyche pieces back together, the adults who can and do remember, withholds important information, denying and fabricating instead of finally doing the right thing and holding up their hands; it is crazy-making as hell. I don't know if this is a big unrealistic ask of perpetrators, but I do know that as a survivor I longed for this particular kind of response and admission, if only to aid me in a fuller recovery by helping me fill in the numbing out-coping mechanism- memory blanks.

I guess that was why Caroline was so keen for us to properly prepare for abuser's most typical line of defence. Like many abusers, he was very cunning, manipulative and crazy-making; it's their bedevilling art. While I was growing up, he had managed to manipulate and fool so many people, most of mother. People thought he was so intelligent, even though he hadn't (successfully) studied at a higher educational level; he was simply awarded his status for his 'gift of gab.'

In hindsight, maybe I would have handled the confrontation, and its preparation, differently, as afterwards, because of his reaction, as strong and adamant as I was, a part of me hadn't been truly ready for the before, during and after experiencing of it all. Having said that, I don't regret confronting him, and I would do it again- and probably the same way. There are things in life that you are never 'ready' for, so you just have to do them, and perhaps this was just one of those.

Thankfully, therapy provided a mirror for all that was and wasn't going on at this level of dissatisfaction that I came to feel so keenly, as well as the resulting and emerging anger. As usual, Caroline saw and understood it all, encouraging me to look at, own, understand, express and therefore release it, rather than put it away, which I had initially and automatically endeavoured to do. The carpet mountain was calling again!

Throughout the weeks that followed, she challenged the desire and the tendency for me to swiftly put it all away, especially the anger. The compulsion to do this was overwhelmingly strong. Holding onto my own perspective and feeling entitled to the full range of my feelings, both past and present, when every other thing inside me just wanted to bury and plaster over it, had been a great big task and a great big ask.

Therapy became desperately hard during this time. There were times when I felt like I got absolutely nothing from the sessions, which left me feeling even more dissatisfied, if that was indeed possible. Then, there was the deep grief, which saw me crying and crying and crying, both in and outside of therapy, although outside of therapy I hid the crying, making sure I held it down and only cried when I was on my own. I couldn't let Jamie see me falling apart, which was what it began to feel like was happening. However, in the midst of these deep feelings and healing, there remained a growing hope and faith; this growing reassurance and consciousness that continued to keep me company and helped keep me keeping on.

BOOK TWO:

INSIDE-OUT

CHAPTER FOUR

Although the abuser stopped coming physically around as much, he stepped up his efforts to turn me back around. He did this mainly by phone, continuing in the same vein and in the same desperation with the same lies. I had been conditioned to forgive what could be deemed unforgivable, and to accept, understand and live with absolutely atrocious behaviour, so it took me a while to finally lose my cool and tell him to sling his fucking hook.

Indeed, it was his constant irresponsible, inconsiderate, irritating and infuriating behaviour that made me decide to disclose all to my mother. If he had behaved otherwise, I might not have chosen to go down that road, but now I felt compelled to do so because I felt that he needed to be properly outed. Hidden in that decision was also the hope that perhaps being outed in front of my mother might bring him to the position he needed to be in, so that at the very least he would have no more justifications and would come to know the wrong he had done, if only so that he may never do it again.

It was time to truly shame the devil, and in addition to it all, I began to feel it was important for my mother to know what it was truly like for me, and what her trusted and still close friend had done to me. For me, this meant a further coming into my own; of bringing closure to not only all the bad conditionings, but also the pretence in my family, all of which seemed really relevant and extremely important to my healing journey.

Preceding the disclosure, I also had a dream in which I was very angry with my sister Beverly, who had been the eldest and therefore the one given the weighty responsibility of being mother to us all in our actual mother's absences. The last time I'd sat my mother down and attempted to have an open and honest discussion with her, Beverly never supported me, nor did she even try to understand why I had wanted to do that. The dream also featured my mother's constant comings and goings, which accounted for the other portion of my anger.

I think I was also very angry at Beverly in the dream, not only because she was a second mummy in command back when we were children, whether I liked it or not, but also because during that time, and over the following years, I felt she had taken advantage of me by expecting me to take care of her children almost every weekend, just like our mother had done to her.

Like the time before, I had chosen to meet with my mother at my house and communicate first-hand through letter. It wasn't as if she had not been expecting this conversation, as some months before she had asked if there was anything on my mind that we needed to talk about, as she had noticed that something was up. This was her way of pointing out that I was changing, and therefore our relationship was no longer the same; I was no longer the pleasing, obedient, agreeable little girl of old. I also believe that her concern was prompted by the fact that I had been in touch with her mother, my Gran, in Jamaica.

The relationship between my mum and Gran was non-existent, a situation that had escalated somewhat after my mother's father died when she was nine years old. Over the years, my mother had openly shared how much she had loved her dad and disliked her mother. My mother felt that Gran was a cold, withholding and rigid woman, who had always put men first, ahead of her daughter; a daughter she had shown very little, if any, love towards. To my mother, Gran was a woman who had offered her one and only child and daughter, and her grandchildren,' little help and support.

From the outset of my written correspondence with Gran, she had received me very warmly and joyfully. During our correspondences, I also picked up on the feeling that she had many regrets, and I thought that with the right kind of help for them both in the way of open, honest, direct and clear communication, things could have been very different. Additionally, through our correspondence, which lasted until her death, it became clear that Granny had ended up very isolated and lonely, with no family and hardly any friends; just God and alcohol in the end. This had left her open and vulnerable to opportunists, who messed with her mail and got in the way of the small amounts of money that I would try and send.

At that time, my mum was showing concern, and, observing

our own estrangement, it would be fair to say that I had felt unsettled by it. In the main, I was unsettled by her concern because I didn't know if I could trust it or her. I didn't know if she was being genuine. I wasn't sure if she was just fishing to see what Granny had and was saying, and in response, I had responded, 'Haven't we always been distant?' before rather coolly following with, 'When I'm ready, we will talk.'

The first part of the letter focused on her behaviour towards me as a child, and spoke of how her actions had impacted me, making me believe that there was something about me to be hated, disliked and left behind, all of which had made me feel very much uncared for and unloved. These feelings lingered in me as adult, and a part of me still desperately felt the need to be heard, seen and reckoned with. Like I said, I was still very angry with her, but in the face of the family denial of the trauma in our past, a part of me still struggled to feel entitled to that anger.

As usually happened whenever I attempted to share my innermost feelings with my mother, I took particular care not to blame her, but to take full ownership of my feelings and just speak on behalf of myself; for the sole purpose of being understood and heard, and the clearing of air. Even in my own pain, I knew that my mother had issues that I didn't want to add to. I just wanted her to hear and know me fully, and finally, though I did at times feel like a very naughty little girl for questioning her.

The second part of the letter shared with her what the abuser had done to me, and by the time I had finished reading it, it seemed that she had put completely out of her mind the parts of the letter that related to her and our relationship specifically.

Instead, and perhaps to a certain extent understandably –
although, to tell you the truth, I couldn't really see it at the time,
and just thought that it was typical of her – she chose to focus
on the abuser's actions as the sole topic of conversation. I, on
the other hand, was more interested in our issues, as those were
within our control to tackle and move on from.

So, I had to keep bringing her back to us and how related
it all was, because if she hadn't left and neglected us so much,
and been overall so uninvolved – not that I used those words
exactly, but ones to similar affect – it might not have happened,
or at the very least she would have noticed something was wrong
and intervened. Unfortunately, though, she either couldn't or
wouldn't see the link, and later on, rather disappointingly, that
inability to piece together and to see wouldn't only apply to her
just 'finding out' about the abuser and needing space and time
to digest it.

Once she had left the building, she managed to reorganise
it all in her mind, once again defensively citing me as the bad
guy blaming her for everything, and once again, in my eyes,
still remaining loyal and true to the tightly held victim position;
the one and only position she seemed comfortable in. She
also insinuated through her lamentations of 'unfairness' and
'injustice,' that the problem must lie with me because no one else
in the family seemed to have been affected by this past that I
kept going on about. All of this spoke to the part of me that was
already feeling bad for having brought the topic up, making me
feel indeed like the trouble-making bad guy for not just leaving it.

Sadly, in spite of the attempts at open and honest

communication, the family's personal and collective denial and resistance to full acknowledgement, healing and growth continued on, so much so that even though the abuser and my mother did initially fall out, within a month or two they were back together as friends. As had been the case in previous confrontations, it was like nothing had happened at all.

I cannot convey the utter dismay, anger and disappointment that I felt a couple of months on, being together at a family gathering for one of the children's birthday and him being there, and everybody seeming to be totally oblivious to the effect that his presence could be having on me. Words cannot describe how terribly re-traumatized, alone, silenced and wronged I had felt at the time.

My mother and the abuser did finally part company a year later, though it wasn't because of what he had done to me, though it was getting increasingly difficult for my mother to put that to the back of her mind since he kept bringing it up, like he did with me, trying to absolve himself of the guilt he should have felt. Ultimately, they parted ways because he repeatedly, and rather jealously, sought to interfere in her love life.

I felt completely let down and unsupported by the various members of my family; feelings that I endeavoured to take into therapy, which wasn't at all easy. Therapy once again became a most difficult place to be, as I struggled to deal with the full range of those feelings, especially the anger and very bitter disappointment. I also found myself, again, equally challenged to resist the massive temptation, which still existed, to run away from myself as a way of escape and dissociation; as a way of managing and coping which had once served me well enough, but was now just getting in the way of my recovery. Being locked within that conflict was excruciating at times.

My dependency on weed also picked up with similar intensity and speed, as did the need to be rid of it because I knew, long-term, it wasn't doing me any good, plus I couldn't really afford it. So, I kept up my efforts to quit, with relative success here and there, but nothing terribly sustained. It also begun to dawn on me most clearly at this time that weed smoking had taken the place of Bulimia. Like Bulimia, it was an attempt at coping and providing some hope; the hope of a better tomorrow in the pursuit of a more effective and perfect spliff that could take me way up high, far away from all this fucking painful shite.

The weed smoking, or not smoking, eventually became an excruciating pain that got tied in with everything else. One problem fed into another, clouding over the bigger picture, slowing progress and adding more disappointment, this time at myself, which turned my anger inwards, rather than appropriately placing and therefore doing away with it. Addictions are crazy-making, however much relief they initially, and temporarily, bring. In this regard, despite how well I was doing, emotionally I felt like I was failing.

From the outside, I continued to look strong, capable and charged. I was by then in the third, going onto last, year of the degree course, and academically, intellectually and appearance-wise, all seemed, and to a certain extent was, well. I was very good at being the intelligent and capable side of myself, with books and learning having acted as inanimate sources of companionship:

support and friendship for as long as I could remember.

In disclosing the sexual abuse to my family, for a time in therapy it felt easier for me to focus my attention on discussing all the men who had taken advantage of me as a child. There had been others, touching me up here and there. In some of these situations, I tried to use the wrong that was happening to my advantage; the advantage being that perhaps I would get some money for food, sweets or dolls, and this became the focus and the hope instead. Having a desired trade-off in mind helped me to live less disturbed by the fact of how taken advantage of I actually was. It dampened the pain and desperation of it all.

Caroline listened with interest and was really sympathetic, but she was also keen for me to think about how my being in those situations came about in the first place. She felt that those things were directly linked to my being neglected, unprotected and abandoned as a child. She also wondered if I was preferring to talk about this particular area in an attempt to avoid the present immense inner turmoil and pain that I was experiencing post-confrontations; the actual situation and difficulty that was currently at hand. She encouraged me to deal more immediately and directly with this particular matter, although she could more than see and understand how awful, desperate, exploitative and wrong those situations had been.

In essence, she felt that in those situations with those men, I was trying to get something from them that I was not getting from my mother, who had left me starving hungry, not only physically, but especially and particularly emotionally, which made absolute sense. However, on some level it still felt and seemed awfully wrong to allow myself to continue with the anger I felt towards my mum, and the painful and bitter disappointment I felt in regard to her lack of presence, both past and now most definitely present.

Deep down, and like I said, doing and being and feeling that way towards her felt like a betrayal her, as though I wasn't honouring thy mother as the Good Book says. I still felt the need to be good and to believe that being so would get me what I wanted, which was another maladaptive trade-off practice that I had taken up in childhood, which never reaped reward.

It seemed easier, more second nature, more familiar to abandon and betray my real deep-down feelings instead. It still felt second nature to want to put my mother's needs above my own, like I was the mother and she was the child. To fully allow this newly developing and unknown side of myself, which I fully understand now was the real me whose development had not been nurtured and nourished, but had instead been arrested, was very hard. The maladapted me, which my mother had regularly fed the food of self-dislike, self-blame and self-doubt in the land of let's pretend, psychologically held tightly to her, albeit unconsciously.

So during this time of self-recovery and self-rediscovery, feeling entitled to legitimate anger still remained a challenge for me. However, during this time, especially after bearing witness to how my family reacted to the disclosures and confrontations, I was truly able to appreciate and understand why I hadn't disclosed the sexual abuse as a child, as much as I wanted to a number of times; like the time when I was eleven years old and I just couldn't stop crying.

Now seeing and realising how wise that decision not tell then was had filled me at this difficult time with a certain amount of comfort, peace, self-respect and self-love. To have dared to disclose the sexual abuse during my childhood, amidst all the family pain and denial, would have been psychological suicide. It would have killed me off far beyond the degree to which I was already dead to the world to begin with, to the point that I would have been unable to ever breathe new life into my mortally wounded self. To have shared would have been too much then; it had to have been now.

Sadly, however, in the midst of all this, disappointment was to raise its ugly head again, in an unexpected turn of events. This came to pass in mid-October when, ten months into the 'open-ended' therapy sessions and two months post-confrontation and disclosure, Caroline announced that she would be leaving the Inner-city Centre. This meant that our work together would have to come to an end in approximately six weeks' time, on 13th December 1991.

Needless to say, I was completely devastated and totally flabbergasted. I couldn't believe what I was hearing when Caroline told me, and I reacted by immediately breaking down in tears. I couldn't even speak for the rest of the session. I didn't want to talk because I didn't want to have to be dealing with this situation – I didn't want it to be real. I had made great progress with Caroline, and we had done some really deep and important work together. Plus, the therapy was supposed to be open-ended, meaning that it was due to last as long as I needed it, which was something I liked and had wanted. I couldn't understand why we were ending.

Caroline never did say exactly why the therapy had to come to that unexpected end, and I never dared or thought long enough to ask why. I didn't think it was allowed, being the maladapted good girl that I inside-out was. I had gotten the feeling that there had been a disagreement and subsequent parting of ways between her and the agency she was employed by, or at least she said and didn't say as much. I didn't feel that she would have made the decision lightly, but boy did it fucking hurt, and yes, I was very angry with her, a feeling that she encouraged me to express and to articulate and own. This was something that I endeavoured to do, but in spite of the permission, I still found it painfully difficult. Besides, it took time to get over the shock of it, let alone to express anger about it.

Alas, before too long, and as automatically as I had done with everything emotionally painful, disappointing and unexpected, I kept thinking, believing and feeling that I should accept and be over it, her leaving now, two weeks in. The familial mountainous carpet turned up, wanting me to sweep more unfinished business under it, and I also kept thinking that Caroline expected that of me, too. To a certain extent, and perhaps more unconsciously, Caroline wanted me to put it away in good time order, to her agenda, if only for herself to feel a bit better about leaving me in such a way and during such a difficult time. I felt this sometimes in the way she wanted me to get straight to the anger I felt and work it through.

During this period of the therapy, amongst other things and feelings, I (unconsciously) kept getting her, and the situation at hand, totally mixed up with my past situation of being abandoned by my mum. It was hugely confusing, but we moved forward and dealt with the reality of the situation head on, and as hard as that was, Caroline remained congruent and consistent. She wouldn't have it any other way, never mind have me deny and bury it, and when we arrived at the very end of the last session, we hugged it out and said our goodbyes. Caroline wouldn't have that any other way, either. Left to my own devices, even though I wanted a hug, I would have just said goodbye and left, but she came in for the hug, and her embrace felt genuine, loving, cosy and warm, however incredibly sad it all was.

BOOK TWO:

INSIDE-OUT

CHAPTER FIVE

During the process of ending therapy, Caroline and I had discussed my finding a new therapist. She was keen that there should be very little pause and that I should definitely continue on, so a replacement was quickly identified. Caroline had done her training with this particular woman, with whom I went to have a consultation and subsequently decided to continue on in therapy with after a three-and-a-half-week break.

I began therapy with Brenda Fletchman-Smith on January 9th 1992. Brenda was an attractive, middle-aged (probably in her mid-to-late forties), well presented and natural-looking black woman, who wore her hair in a short afro. She held sessions in her home, where she made use of a couch, which I hadn't experienced before. I was quite impressed with the set-up, and had thought that I would like to aspire one day to what she had managed to create here for herself. My first impression was that she was a kind of an inspiration, particularly because she was a black woman. I'd never worked with a black therapist before.

I liked using the couch, as for me it took away the shame, embarrassment and inhibition I sometimes felt making and maintaining eye-to-eye contact. Using the couch better enabled me to speak more freely, without worrying about how the therapist was receiving me and what I was saying. It also gave me a certain confidence to talk about difficult things, as well as voice discontent, even towards Brenda, as it was quite a process getting used to working with her and getting used to the fact that I had to change therapists. Somewhere inside, I was still very angry at the injustice of having to finish up with Caroline before the agreed time and having to start all over again. Those unhappy feelings became more apparent with time.

Brenda was so much different in style and character than Caroline had been. It took some getting used to, perhaps in the same way it had taken some getting used to as a child having to adjust time and again to the different personality styles of the various others I stayed with in my mother's absence. In regard to Brenda, from the first time we met in the consultation, I didn't like and never got used to her referring to me as a 'patient.' It made me feel defective and small, and to me showed her as wanting to appear as the expert and one in charge.

The therapy was also a bit more expense at £15 a session, and as a result I was back to one session per week. A part of me couldn't help but feel cheated and tricked. Brenda had also said that once I finished studying the fees would go up to £20, and then £25 once I started work, which was at the time her actual going rate. All of this I initially and immediately felt uncomfortable with, as money was already tight, but she didn't seem to be too open to negotiation around fees.

Even at the best of times, Brenda felt overly precise, professional, parental and no-nonsense, which made me feel uncomfortable from the outset, although I put it away and chose to work with her anyway – I think more to please Caroline than anything else. However, several weeks into the sessions, in regard to compatibility, I began to wonder if I should have shopped around a bit more; I began to wonder if I had made the right choice for me, for on a level something about her – an aggressiveness, or perhaps her no-nonsense assertiveness – unnerved me.

Like I said, Brenda's style, manner and way of working was very different than Caroline's. Brenda's was more of a tough kind of love, and a lot of the time, at least for the first three months, the sessions felt terribly disjointed, and had me wandering just how much Caroline had fed back to Brenda about me. It didn't seem like Caroline had fed back anything and it was as though Brenda and I were totally starting from scratch, and I hated it. I hated starting again from scratch; that was not where I felt I needed to be or where I felt sessions should have been at this point.

Brenda had her own way in regard to how she saw things and what she chose to draw my attention to, and for us to 'look at.' Sometimes, it felt like this was exactly as she liked and wanted it, with herself being in total charge of the therapeutic process. When I tried to express my thoughts and feelings of dissatisfaction, it seemed she would chastise me. For example, when I voiced concerns around fees and tried so see if it could be reduced to £10 a session, she would not have it. She said that my previous therapist(s) had 'infantilised' me by allowing me to have therapy at reduced fees. At the time, and particularly in regard to fees, I truly felt misunderstood by what she had said, and felt like it was her who was treating me like a child with the force-feed of her opinions.

Brenda also made me feel like I was asking or expecting too much in regard to other things. For instance, when I used to talk about my family, feeling like I was making good progress here because I was giving better vent to my anger regarding situations with them, continuing from where Caroline and I had left off, she would seem to show a certain disdain and would become bit irritated and impatient. She'd say things to the effect of that my family is not in therapy, so we can't do anything about them, and that perhaps my time would be better spent focusing on myself, which would make me feel chastised again.

Brenda also called me arrogant once, saying that I was in the habit of placing people above or below me. She also said that I was in the habit of playing victim, a role she felt was seductive to me, almost insinuating, and at times directly suggesting, that I should grow up, move on and take more responsibility for myself as an adult.

I didn't always get Brenda. Her interpretations made me feel guilty, like I was using the past to avoid taking responsibility for myself today, and that I was not willing to look at the part I played in things, instead wallowing in self-pity. And little while down the road, when I mentioned my weed smoking, she was keen to zoom in on that; in on the fact that I smoke even though I couldn't afford it. She was clear that I should give it up, arguing that smoking stops the things I am learning, especially in the therapy situation, from becoming useful to me. She made it crystal clear that she felt my smoking to be destructive and sabotaging and that it had no place in the therapeutic process of change.

Some of the things she said, and the way that she said them, did piss me off, mainly because it felt like she was trying to push me in a direction that I wasn't ready or able to go in, even though I knew it would be on the agenda when I was ready, just like I had dealt with the eating disorder and other issues before. It just felt at times that it was all about Brenda and Brenda's agenda, like how it had felt with my mother.

I mean, to give her credit, I could see the element of truth that these and her other interpretations held, but it was the way she presented it and herself that hadn't gone down particularly well. Perhaps her style would have been more helpful and beneficial if I had met Brenda at a later date along the road of growth and change.

We did go on to address and work through the anger, disappointment and abandonment I felt at Caroline's departure, which had helped. For my part, in the therapeutic encounter with Brenda, I did feel that bit more able to be with and express my anger and dissatisfaction, even towards her. During our last session, Caroline had said to me, 'Make sure that your next therapist takes care of you,' and I had kept to that. I was holding Caroline's words, not only due to the couch and the freedom of expression it seemed to encourage, but because Brenda was pissing me off, so I made her know it; 'it' seeming to be the saying of exactly how I was thinking and feeling in any and every given situation, which had felt very naughty and out of character for me, but at the same time, deep inside, had also felt incredibly healthy.

I don't know to what exact extent Brenda being black, and reminding me of my mother in certain respects, negatively affected or detracted from things, but I do know that it had a significant impact, which had taken me by surprise. I still made the best of the sessions, and at a certain point felt that I had settled into them and that she and I were really working, even if we didn't always see eye to eye. Plus, overall, I still admired and respected Brenda, however more aggressive, honest and direct she was than Caroline. I can work with, and live with, honest and direct, more so than denial and deceptiveness.

It was during the therapeutic encounter with Brenda that I made my first serious and sustained effort to give up smoking weed, not long after I had initially brought it up in the session and she had reacted as she had. I managed to stop for four weeks, and even after resuming, continued cutting down. However, I didn't tell Brenda immediately when I started smoking again; I only told her when I had stopped. Cutting down was difficult enough, as being without the crutch and coping mechanism of weed smoking put me in more direct contact with painful feelings of desperation, neediness and deep loneliness. In turn, these painful feelings made more urgent the need to be in weed smoking company, such was the vicious cycle it had become.

Another important thing that Brenda helped me bring into clearer consciousness, even though after that point it still took some time getting used to, as well as some putting into practise, was the whole arena of dating. The subject came up as I was sharing with her experiences regarding this guy I had met and had been seeing and getting to know, mainly through him coming to my house and us chatting and sharing each other's company, as well as a spliff. His name was Larry, and we had been seeing each other, without actually going out of the house, for some weeks before I brought it to the sessions.

I brought it to the sessions because Larry was, as it turned out, giving me mixed messages, as well as putting pressure on me to take the relationship, or more accurately the 'situation,' to another level. I had been single and celibate for quite some time by then, two years to be exact, and had had my doubts about Larry and how I really felt about him. I had some concerns about him and his true intentions, though these remained unacknowledged and unexpressed, until I raised the issue with Brenda that is. Brenda helped me to see that he was indeed sending out mixed messages, and that by all I had told her he'd said, and the way he behaved, that it sounded very much to her like he was already in relationship and living with someone.

It was during this conversation that I realised that I didn't actually know what dating was, let alone how to go about it. My habitual way of getting together with someone had been swift, easy and quick, with little or no courting or wooing. My availability had all been too obvious, and my judgment impaired on the basis that I didn't give myself enough time to get to know my suitors and find out whether they were truly a good match for me. I hadn't even seen it done during my childhood; I had only seen the form of dating that I had been emulating.

I hadn't looked at it like that before, the way Brenda was getting me to consider now. I thought that was the way it was, and at that point realised that there was so much I didn't know in regard to intimacy, love and relationships. At this time in the therapy, I was able to take more on board the 'seductive victim role' that Brenda had mentioned before, which I did tend to get caught up in. I could see in particular that there was a part I played within it, for better or worse…

For the better, I had the control and power to set boundaries, to be respected and to settle for nothing less. For worse, I perpetrated being taken advantage of by not doing and being those things, and not taking that care of myself. If anything, I was expecting the man to do all of this on my behalf; to naturally just treat me well without my enforcing or establishing it as a prerequisite. By looking more squarely at this issue, I began to see where I was falling short; I began to truly *see* the part that I inadvertently play in the conditions and quality of my life.

It was a great big lesson. I had never seen it that clearly before, and not as clearly as the day I turned up at one of the sessions complaining about how men were looking at me, which I had inferred as disrespectful. Brenda, in her own unique way, put it to me that perhaps if I didn't want or like that kind of attention, that I shouldn't wear short skirts; that I have control, power and influence. Perhaps this is what she had meant in the beginning about growing up, as well as partaking in and of a certain present-day acceptance and working with how things are (some men thinking with the wrong faculty) and taking responsibility for myself and my place in this world knowing this (my words, her leanings).

Like I said, it was some kind of a revelation realising that I had power and control, and it was enlightening to learn that I had a right to my wants, my needs, my feelings, my opinions and my views, just like Brenda had a right to hers, which she exercised unequivocally, unhesitatingly, passionately and explicitly. She had some balls on her!

I was beginning to see how the mistreatment of me as a child had positioned me in life generally, and in mind and body, fundamentally. I was beginning to see *the way* how those early and traumatic childhood experiences had detrimentally given me, in my then and real helplessness and powerlessness, the potential to grow up and entertain a victim or villainous stance. In being able to see this potential occurrence, my thinking brought into view from the other side of the coin, how certain others in their childhoods, who have usually once told themselves, 'I will never be anyone's victim again,' go on to destructively work through their pain by occupying the role of villain later on…Hurt people hurt people - or themselves.

I could better understand the link between past victims and present villains, but this growing knowledge was like a bud that would need much more time to bloom and grow; that would need much more time to take root and hold and come into its own. Inevitably, the situation with Larry came to an abrupt end, especially once I began to take a certain responsibility over myself. During this time, he too fully came into bloom, showing his true murky, menacing and abusive colours.

I really think that Larry believed he was going to play me and get his feet well and truly under the table. Shit, his weed wasn't even that good, and I think he felt extra pissed that he had to share his spliffs with me for as long as he did without some kind of payoff. I believe that he was very much used to, and into, women who did not know their true worth and power, and using them to get ahead himself, being the life-sucking vampire that he was.

During my time with Brenda, I successfully completed my degree course and was considering doing a master's on the subject of eating disorders, which Brenda was keen to encourage me towards. However, after some consideration, I decided that it would be better to get a job and build up a better cash-flow, and once I shared my decision with Brenda, she became very keen to encourage me to get into 'the world of work,' as she had put it, sooner rather than later. When she felt that I wasn't moving as fast as she felt I could in that direction, she took it as a sign that I was having a problem doing so, which I didn't believe to be the case at all. I had been studying hard for five long years, and now wanted to enjoy some free time and space. I wanted to take my good time in looking for work. I hadn't even graduated yet!

Brenda's zealousness in this regard had been a disappointment to me, especially because we had worked together on how difficult 'being' and 'relaxing' were for me, and here she was truly bending my arm to sooner rather than later secure employment. It wasn't that I hadn't been keeping my eyes open for a job; I just wasn't searching as hard or as urgently as she wanted me to be doing.

Then, not too long afterwards, Brenda one day informed me that she would be increasing my fee from the following week, and that when we resumed in September after the summer break, she would be raising the fees up to £25. Just before that time – or around or during, I'm not too sure – she had 'discovered' that I hadn't totally given up smoking weed, so I think she was trying to make a point in that regard, too.

When I tried to discuss with her the possibility of another way of spreading cost, like me coming fortnightly, she said that if I couldn't afford therapy, I should acknowledge that fact and perhaps stop coming altogether until I could afford to pay for it. It wasn't that she said it in a cold-hearted way, but it was quite direct and matter-of-fact. Part of me did somewhat reluctantly see her point, but at the time it pissed me right off!

This was another of what I felt to be her tough love techniques, which I had found quite hard to deal with. Perhaps she also felt she could do this, and suggested it, because she had from the outset said that this would be the case. Perhaps she also took this stance because just before that time, within the therapy, I had gone through a 'quiet stage,' as though I had run out of things to say and to share. At the time, she had referred to it as 'therapy fatigue.' However, the anger towards Brenda and her thoughts and opinions remained. I had felt rejected, and when I discussed the situation with a friend from university, to make sure that I wasn't overacting, she too felt that Brenda was being rather insensitive and unkind.

So, when we broke for the summer, with me owing her £20, I had half-decided to end the sessions, which I shared with Brenda, and which she said we could begin working towards upon my return. When I returned in the September, still jobless, but not troubled by it because I knew it would only be a matter of time, and like I said, I hadn't even graduated yet, I only came back and did two more sessions, which was far from an ending. I left owing her £45, which to date I've never paid. It felt right not doing so, like payback for her not treating me right and forcing me to leave.

Looking back on this therapeutic encounter, as well as overall, Brenda and I did do some important reparative work together. She did help me to take back a certain responsibility and control over myself and my life, which created a major shift in me; a major shift in how I started to view relationships and my place in the world. Considering how our relationship started, with its bittersweet beginnings, we still managed to work through stuff and accomplish a lot, so I'll give Brenda some credit where credit is due, even though there's a side of me that still doesn't want to.

BOOK THREE:

THE BITTER WITH THE SWEET

CHAPTER ONE

"*If God is for me, who can be against me?*"
Romans 8:31

I hated filling in application forms, as selling yourself is a hard thing to do when you struggle with self-esteem issues. However, I remember putting my heart and soul into it, as I really wanted the job I was going for at the time. The position was for a project manager to help run an alcohol counselling service for black women and their families. It sounded just right for me, what with it being part-time, eighteen hours per week, and just up the road from me. I had already done some alcohol counselling during my placement, and at £18,000 pro rota, the salary was appealing, too.

I said a prayer as I posted the completed application form, as I often did when I really wanted something, a habit I got into as a child, and a week and a half later, I was so excited and overjoyed to receive acknowledgement in the post that the application had been successful. I was really happy because I had feared, post-Brenda, that I would have been unemployed for ages, and here I was, second application and first job I had seen and felt that I really wanted, and the application had been successful. At the same time, I tried to keep my head about me and not to get too carried away with it all, as I still had the interview to contend with, which brought its own particular challenges.

The idea of being in a room of strangers, with them asking key questions and me having to come up with the right responses, brought out the jitters in me – jitters that made me feel like a frightened little child at the mercy of some interrogating, dominating and threatening authority figure, who held the power to give or withdraw something very much crucial and needed. Interviews felt emotionally jarring to me.

Old fears of possible and imminent rejection were being stirred up; fears of not being wanted or considered not good enough; fears of making a mistake and getting the answer wrong and looking like such a fool; old fears born out of past realities of oftentimes being made to feel that I was always coming up short on the parental and other authority figures' measuring sticks. However, a more recent, and most definitely corrective, experience of studying and successfully passing my degree gave me a certain confidence, reassurance and encouragement in spite of the fears; all of which accompanied me into the interview situation, giving me the courage that I needed.

The interview went surprisingly well, meaning I felt quite

confident within myself and fairly at ease with all the questioning. I left the interview feeling that all had went well, a feeling that was confirmed later on during the week by phone call and letter offering me the position, which I obviously accepted. I was so happy!

All felt very much on track in my world; the track I had initially set off on with the decision I made in 1982 to have a child and give him and me a second chance, to the renewed decision I made in 1986 to enter therapy and return to higher education and more fully and successfully turn that improved life chances corner. It felt at that time that the job, the degree and the letting go of bulimia, as well as of certain relationships, notwithstanding the growing inner peace, joy and confidence I had been feeling more often than not, were all visible signs of victory; the fruits of all the very real, very hard and harrowing work I had put into my life and self to that date. It was like a beautiful spring morning inside myself when I started work in February 1993, happily embracing the total experience of getting up and going to work, and the purpose, routine and structure it brought into my world.

At first, I had assumed that the work would have entailed some kind of induction process. Not that I had done this kind of work before, but I kind of instinctively knew that ideally something of the sort should have been in place. What was in place was a brief introduction to the service, explaining how and why it had been developed, and where it was in its development in the greater scheme of things.

The Black Women's Alcohol Counselling Service (BWACS) had been developed as a specialised service to meet the growing needs of black women with drinking problems. It was a voluntary sector service and the first specialised alcohol service in the borough. The project coordinator, Martha Jones, had researched and argued for the need of such a service provision, to address the unmet needs of this particular group in the community, and the funding application had been successful.

The need for the BWACS, and the specialist category it was borne out of, related to the (social) fact that even though the black communities comprised a significant percentage of the borough's population, and were seen to be very much in need, they were not accessing the various preventative or other therapeutic services that could help them in their particular and stressful life situations-a situation still unresolved and prevalent today

The programmes that the African, Caribbean and Asian communities tended to occupy the most, and very disproportionately at the chronic, acute and crisis ends, were mental hospitals, social services, prisons and the like. The main argument as to why this situation existed was in that it was a result of institutional racism, therefore, BWACS had to work with and also try to resolve and address these larger social issues wherever it can.

Having been briefed on all of this, I was keen, as the newly appointed project manager, to make a mark and play an important part. I wanted to make a difference and ensure that BWACS went from strength to strength, and as such, realise its full and true potential. This became my focus and passion at work, and it was also a daunting task, as BWACS hadn't built up its client base yet; the project was still very much in its infancy-

perhaps even pregnancy.

Martha seemed a nice enough woman. She was an attractive Dominican, full- figure and in her mid-to-late fifties with her fair share of problems, which she happily shared with me. Although she was easy enough to get along with at first, she was seemingly resistant to letting me get on with things, which started to become somewhat puzzling to me.

As I attempted to break out of and away from Martha's counsel me grip, as well as the menial tasks she would scrape together and give me, I instinctively knew that I had to tread softly and be mindful not to rock the boat too forcefully. So I went about my business, trying to find my way without stepping on toes and bringing myself any unnecessary woes.

In time I came to realise that Martha was not a paid worker, though she was the project's coordinator as well as chairperson on the management committee. Within her varied role it was also her responsibility to write the various progress reports and feedback to the management committee, ensuring that things were functioning well and ticking over smoothly. And in time, and in my efforts to improve the service provisions, questions in time had to be asked, which Martha generally wasn't happy to be put in the position to answer, which obviously left me further confused and increasingly suspicious.

The more I questioned inconsistencies, Martha began pointing the finger of fault at me, trying to make me out to be liar and project destroyer; going on to tell some out and out lies, both to my face and in front of the whole management committee, which was totally humiliating. The majority of people on the management committee were more like her friends, and being blinded as such, naturally leaned towards her side of her story without fully looking into mine.

Thankfully, there were two other committee members who didn't quite know who to believe, but were professional and objective enough not to take sides or jump to any conclusions. It had been a totally stressful, disillusioning and painfully disappointing time for me, and far from what I had excepted when I had first come into post. I felt additionally let down and betrayed by the majority of the committee members for placing me in the situation to begin with. As a management committee and governing body, they had recruited me, and now here they were not protecting me at all. This particular experience had most definitely turned out to be a nightmare scenario come true. But I stood strong in the knowledge of 'what's-done-in-the-dark-must-come-to-light' truth, with the most incriminating piece of evidence, finding me.

There was no getting around this particular bit of evidence, all laid out in black and white before the eyes, which would most definitely bring her wrong very much to light. It concerned a letter she had sent to BWACS' funding body, requesting that they cease the funding as to her mind the project wasn't working and that it wasn't meeting its targets, so therefore it would be in the project's and their best interest to close it down. By then, I had been in post almost four months.

The letter itself was two weeks old, and needless to say, I took copies of it and brought them, along with a couple of other incriminating documents, to the next committee meeting. Not too long after that incident, further incriminating icing on the cake came in the way of a bounced salary cheque, which had bounced even though we had not too long ago received the second quarter of funding. Having the cheque bounce had also at the time truly put me out, as I had had bills desperately waiting to be paid, and cheques that I had written that would now bounce themselves as I waited for it all to be sorted out.

Upon visiting the bank during my lunch break, expecting to withdraw funds and finding out that the cheque had bounced, I went immediately back to work to find out what exactly was going on, whereupon Martha became visibly panicked and upset. She immediately began pleading with me not to say anything to anybody, and to give her some time to sort it out. *I didn't think so!* Just a few days before she had coldheartedly told more lies to my face, as well as within the emergency committee meeting convened concerning 'the letter.' So, I was already fuming regarding her lies and the second meeting they had held in my absence, which had made me feel snubbed.

I was so enraged at her, and at her friends for still even then entertaining a shadow of a doubt of all that had been unjustly said about me. Anyway, the bounced cheque was her just dessert. I owed her no loyalties; she herself had more than seen to that. So she got served and she got out, with four of her management committee cronies following close behind. It was then left up to me to pick up the pieces, or to at least try. I had to fight first and foremost to regain the confidence of the funders, which at the time wasn't easy.

With the support of the remaining committee members, I

wrote the required reports, held the necessary meetings and put across the important message and reasons why BWACS should continue on. I didn't know I had it in me. Perhaps, on another level, I was also fighting for the me that once wasn't allowed to be and grow; perhaps I was also unconsciously and narratively settling old scores of injustices, all of which felt challenging, but somehow much easier to see through and carry out in a workplace situation.

Thankfully, the funding body decided to give us another chance. We had two months to not only continue to prove ourselves and the need for the service, but also to put into place and account for other much needed things, like a new bank account, the securing of new premises, electing more committee members and coming up with new aims, objectives and targets, as well as monitoring and evaluation procedures, etc.

It was during this process of putting into place and securing all these things, and awaiting the funding body's final decision, that I met Chris. It was June 1993, although it felt and seemed like I had been working at BWACS for at least a couple of years! I must say, at the time, meeting Chris had felt like a most welcome and timely distraction.

BOOK THREE:

THE BITTER WITH THE SWEET

CHAPTER TWO

I used to often walk past Chris's shop, Orisha, which sold cultural artefacts, like Afrocentric books about Black African and Caribbean history and culture, as well as greeting cards, clothes, paintings, statutes and other ornamental bits. The shop was just down the road from me and I had started to walk past and make more use of it after I started doing my post-graduation voluntary counselling work at Mind. Generally, I used to go into the shop to buy greeting cards and incense sticks, and to browse the books, which was a tendency that increased after going in there one day and noticing this rather attractive man, who also noticed me.

He was really quite striking and of good build, standing at least six-foot. His complexion was cocoa-coloured, dark, with deeply set dimpled cheeks and these big round eyes and a bright sunshine smile. He also wore the various African Kente cloths, tops and hats, which gave him a certain regal vibe, all of which made me think and feel that if he was interested in getting to know me, that I was interested in him, too. It was a really exciting time, as I had been celibate and without romantic interests for more than three years.

During one of my visits to the shop, Chris and I had gotten into a really interesting conversation, about what my mind does not recall. All I know is that he talked and when I talked, he listened! He heard what I was saying and responded in all the right places, and to top it all off, the shop remained customer-free the whole time, which seemed like ages, and as though time had literally stood still for us. After our conversation, he asked if I would like to go to the cinema the following Friday, to which I had said yes. When I left the shop, my head was in the clouds and I was ever so excited. Friday couldn't come soon enough, but I was satisfied to have the memory of our discourse to keep me in good company until we met again.

It was through my association with Chris that I got into the Black Consciousness Movement (BCM), which I believe went on to move me into a more expanded and historically true sense of identity; a movement that helped me to take the adage 'know thyself' to totally new levels. BCM taught me a way of looking, seeing and understanding life in a way that puts the black and African experience back in its original and rightful place, before its more positive influences and essence became so totally denigrated, contaminated and replaced with all sorts of ***other-than-we- are*** ways.

On the personal plane, (for both black & white people

alike), there's still a lot to be discovered, recovered, learned and unlearned, ahead of being forgiven. And at the macroscopic scale of things, to truly achieve a more complete forgiveness of the wrongs done to black folks and their once richly resourced culture and key contributions on the world stage, much still needs to be acknowledged and repaired to enable true reparation to take its place. Reparation, much more than, 4 acres and a mule...

My particular re-education in this all-important area as a person of African-Caribbean descent took root right there, and over the years culminated in the beginning of a spiritual awakening that worked towards me becoming ever so proud and grounded in that ancestry. I read many books on Afrocentric themes, so hungry and thirsty did I become for those teachings, all of which Chris happily, willingly and freely fed me.

Like never before did the colour of my skin make me feel anything but complete; never before had I been more ready, willing and able to challenge inferiority and superiority 'complexes' coming from within and without, now that I knew how beautiful, skilful and truly integral to world history black/Nubian people were and are. I embrace that fact in delight and reverence.

The day of our first date arrived, and I was both tremendously nervous and excited. I wore my locks down, with the front bit pulled up and falling back on itself. I also wore a little bit of makeup – just the basics of some foundation, eyeliner, mascara, and a little lipstick. I didn't need much makeup as my skin tone had its own natural and vibrant glow, being a copper-coloured reddish brown, which gave me a certain Egyptian mysteriousness in regards to cultural heritage, Nefertiti-style.

At this time, I was still very much psychologically growing into my looks, having grown up believing myself to be ugly and unattractive, but on good days I knew I was a sight to behold, like I was the night of that first date. That night, I wore a black mini skirt that fell just above the knees, with a red top and a short waist-length black leather jacket, and big round gold earrings; colours and styles that complimented me while also highlighting other assets.

The date turned out to be a double date, with his mate and his girlfriend coming along, and I remember thinking that I would have much preferred it if it had been just the two of us. We went to the pictures in Leicester Square, West End, but while I don't recall what film we watched, I do remember, most definitely and clearly, what Chris told me as we were having drinks just before going in to see the movie; he told me that he was married.

I was absolutely dumbfounded, disappointed and confused. I remember thinking, *Why ask me on a date, then?* Actually, at first I had thought I didn't hear him right, so had to ask him to repeat himself, which he did, going on to say that he wanted to be up front and honest with me about his marital status. He said that it wasn't fair not to let me know or to lead me on, *but hadn't he already done that?!*

I didn't understand. I didn't know what he expected me to say. I didn't even know whether I should have kept the smile frozen on my 'fool you' face, a smile that remained to cover up the pure and total disappointment and embarrassment I felt. Somehow, right or wrong, I then felt I had to be 'big' about it – mature and stuff; that I had to be seen to take it on the chin like the adult I was. After all, I was already out with him.

On the drive back, I continued to appear outwardly happy and friendly, but inside I was still confused and filled with question, as I endeavoured to keep the disappointment- which was ready to spill over, at bay. I so fancied him, and had hoped that my time for love had come, but what he had told me was the very last thing I'd wanted, or indeed expected, to hear.

Chris broke the silence by saying words to the effect of that he didn't want me to think badly of him; it's just that he is very attracted to me and very much would still like to get to know me and see where things between us leads. Rightly or wrongly, Chris saying all this had felt a little comforting: like perhaps all was not lost and there still was some hope. So I went along with what he had said, and with the fact that I still cared for certain other promising aspects of his personality, which was new to me in my then dating history. I decided that I would continue to see him, for now.

Luckily, a month into the relationship, and totally off his own back, he did separate from his wife, which made me very happy and caused me to decide to hang around, thinking that perhaps I was still onto something good. At around the same time, I received word from the funders that our rescue mission for BWACS had been successful, and that they would be happy to continue to fund us, which had been really great news.

Financially, things also improved somewhat, as Chris gave me some money here and there, provided takeaways and supplied the weed – little things that made a favourable financial difference.

As time went on, the relationship went from strength to strength, and I truly came to enjoy being with him. We got along like a house on fire. Chris was understanding, attentive, caring and supportive, just to list a few of his attributes, and he also had a great sense of humour. I hadn't laughed as much in years, and Jamie also warmed and took very well to him.

Having successfully secured further funding, BWACS moved into a community project building. The new coordinator and chair, Janet Summers, also ran, within the same community of projects, a women's organisation. She had already been on the BWACS management committee, and was one of the few who had truly supported me throughout the Martha ordeal.

I liked being in this new space. It was a big community house that, along with BWACS and Janet's organisation, housed a number of community-based projects, all of which were utilised and accessed well. It was truly a 'happening place' that had a renaissance liberation feel to it, and it felt really good being there. It also felt really good to finally be left to my own devices. It was great being trusted to get on with things and endeavour to bring BWACS into greater being.

The work was both challenging and fulfilling; challenging because we were starting from scratch and, like already mentioned, being a specialist service, we were also in competition with other mainstream service providers. As a result, we were always under constant pressure to prove ourselves; to prove that there was a need and that we were getting the numbers in.

Overall, I enjoyed the BWACS experience. I enjoyed developing it, I enjoyed putting all it needed to run effectively and

smoothly into place, I enjoyed writing and presenting my ide.
at the monthly committee meetings and I also enjoyed setting up
the required outside supervision and support networks for myself.
Getting clients in the door was a much less straightforward task,
so much so that I began to wonder if alcohol was in fact 'the
problem' that was affecting black family life, and whether the
black community themselves saw it as a problem at all. However,
in the face of all that, I continued on with high hopes.

During that year of 1993, Jamie had started the final year
of primary school and overall had been doing well, although
not working to his full potential, as his school report oftentimes
mentioned. However, I wasn't unduly concerned, as in terms of
personality and well-being, he was still very much a well-adjusted
and happy boy, and we still enjoyed a free and easy mother-son
relationship; these things were my first and foremost. Jamie was
also a keen football player, and as well as playing for his school
football team, was also playing for an under-eleven Sunday
league team, an arrangement that went on until he was fifteen
years old.

When Chris and I started going out, Chris became the one
who took us to the weekly Sunday league matches and other
tournaments and games. It was a real special time, the whole
Chris, us and football experience. I had really gotten into football
at the time, not being able to go to bed on Saturday nights until I
had watched Match of the Day highlights.

I used to truly enjoy watching Jamie's games, shouting
out support and encouragement from the side-lines without
inhibition, and perhaps also trying to make up for the fact that his

father never came to see him play. Chris truly made a difference in this regard, encouraging and praising Jamie, and even giving him money whenever he scored a goal.

Jamie really liked Chris; they got on really well together. Their relationship was, much like Chris's and mine, and Jamie and me, an easy one. Chris was like a big kid himself sometimes, and he would crack Jamie and I up in fits of laughter when the spirit took him. Jamie grew quite close to him, which was something I hadn't realised until Christmas of the same year. I had finally got the Christmas that I had spent all of my life wanting and craving: happy family, together and enjoying one another's company. The day was wonderful and truly filled with cheer, with Chris, as usual, cracking his jokes, and it was in the midst of all that that I had taken a step back and got a snap shot of just how happy everybody was, especially my son, which warmed and filled my little cotton socks no end. This was how it went for a time, until the summer of the following year, when Chris decided to go back to his wife.

I was truly amazed that after all we had shared and had come to mean to each other, he could have still made that particular decision. It was such a disappointing blow, as I really liked him, indeed loved him, and so did Jamie. We had all worked and got along so well, but in my heart, I knew, or perhaps more feared, that as long as he was still married, he might one day decide to reunite with his wife. In my heart of hearts, I also knew what I must do if such decision came to pass.

I don't think he knew or realised that I only finally decided to remain in the relationship with him after he had left his wife.

If he hadn't, after a certain period of time, I would have had to call it a day. I had already been there and done that in previous relationships prior to celibacy and Chris, and I couldn't go back there again; that would have been like going backwards. Three-way relationships just didn't work for me, not even the no strings attached, cheap thrill side of it. To me, someone always ends up getting hurt, and usually the one who comes in last is the first to go.

Sadly, it wasn't until a little while afterward that I realised how much the break-up had impacted Jamie. We were having a conversation, and he said words to the effect of, 'What's the point in getting married? People just break up anyway. I'm never getting married.' I guess the events of Chris and I, and the subsequent end of the relationship between the two of them, reawakened in Jamie old past wounds of loss; the loss experienced in the break up between his father and I and the end as we knew it of our little family.

Jamie still had a relationship with his father, who did take him out fairly regularly, albeit sporadically. However, it wasn't an emotionally close and relaxed relationship any more, not like it had been with Chris. It was more an idealised one.

Jamie's then thoughts about relationships made me feel bad, because in all of it, from the beginning of the Chris experience to the very end, I had forgotten, once again, to consider Jamie and his needs. Jamie's somewhat despairing and pessimistic statement about relationships had sent a certain shudder through me, making me wander how in future these particular key experiences would go on to shape him, particularly in his own love life. The thought made me feel guilty, like a not-too-good, once again, blindsided, mummy.

BOOK THREE:

THE BITTER WITH THE SWEET

CHAPTER THREE

During the summer of 1994, after the break-up with Chris, came the resurgence of old painful feelings of discontent, emptiness, sadness and loneliness. Work continued to be a struggle, and although I had made great strides, now seeing a handful of clients, I was beginning to feel as if I had come to the end of something with BWACS too. The workload was far too great, and I could see no end to it; no light at the end of the tunnel. I guess I was also extremely tired emotionally and otherwise. I didn't feel like I wanted or needed to prove myself at BWACS anymore.

Finances also began to become a bit of a struggle again, as did my dependence on weed. As I got caught back up in smoking, old feelings of guilt, disappointment, neediness and greed resurfaced, especially when I gave in to the need for weed, and bought it knowing full well that I couldn't really afford it, and that in the long term it was doing me much more harm than good. I just knew I had to give it up, and that it couldn't be part of my healing journey as trying to cope with and regulate my difficult feelings in this way, kept me tied to a painful, *anger-turned-in-on-itself,* self-blaming past.

Fortunately, in the midst of all this came a great job opportunity with a service I had outreached at before as part of BWACS's developmental process, where I had met with its new project manager, Barbara Wright. The organisation was called Intentions, and it was based in South London. It was a new project on new premises that were newly furnished, providing an alcohol recovery centre for people from the black community, which was the first of its kind in London. Its remit, and reason for development, was similar to BWACS, only it was operating on a much larger scale and with a more financially secure base.

Intentions was the brain child of a well-established voluntary service provision, delivering not only alcohol counselling for problem drinkers, but also housing, drop-ins, group work and other related services within a number of different boroughs, with Intentions being its latest initiative. In the third year of the Psycho-Social degree course, I had also done one of my placements at one of its other projects, the Women's Alcohol Centre, so I was already quite familiar with the organisation and how it worked, as well as with its approach to problem drinking, and its aims and objectives.

I remember the first time I visited Intentions, and how impressed I had been with its décor and how well adorned the premises were, with the display of pictures, positive quotes and other cultural artefacts that presented well and spoke to the community which it served. Being in the centre, I had definitely felt welcome and warm. It was just so fresh and new; so very full of potential. Being there had felt like a vocation homecoming for me.

I had joked with Barbara at the time how very envious I felt, as Intentions made BWACS seem more like a welfare case. It was so roomy, spacey and well equipped, with a dedicated, 28-hour-a-week admin worker and a pool of volunteers to draw from. I had wished then that I was a part of it. For her part, Barbara had seemed nice enough; she was willing to learn, and I was willing to share with her all that I knew, since she was new to both the alcohol counselling field and her role as project manager.

A month or so after our first meeting, Barbara called to inform me that Intentions was recruiting for a full-time alcohol counsellor/advice worker, and asked if I would be interested in applying. Rather spontaneously, and surprising even myself, I had jumped at the chance and said yes. So, I applied, was shortlisted, went on to interview and subsequently got the job.

The position was full-time and paid £17,500-£21,500 per annum, which I was more than overjoyed with. For the first time in a long time, it seemed that money would no longer be tight as it was. I was also overjoyed at the general prospect of working at Intentions, and totally excited at being a part of such a new and innovative project developed to serve the (unmet) needs of the black communities. I was truly up for being at the forefront of that kind of initiative, as well as a challenge that actually seemed to stand more of a fighting chance.

Barbara was ecstatic that I got the post, and I was looking forward to working with her. Like I said, she seemed really nice: eager to please, laid back and fun-loving. I was very grateful because getting that job had been and seemed like a dream come true; like I was still progressing nicely in the land of (my) dreams.

It had been quite difficult giving in notice at BWACS, which had been my baby; one that had almost lost its life before I stepped in and saved it. I had really enjoyed being a part of BWACS, and it had shaped me professionally, but there was no denying the fact that Intentions was a great opportunity and met all of my current needs, so as hard as it was to leave BWACS, I knew it was time, and also a good move for my own professional development. The idea of being better supported, and not being a project's all and everything, brought with it a comforting feeling, and I couldn't wait to see how that situation actually felt.

Intentions had a lot going for it; its future was brighter and much more secure. These were the reasons I gave to Janet as to why I was leaving, and even though she was sad to have to see me go, she understood and was supportive. Before I left, I endeavoured to ensure that BWACS had as good a handover as was humanly possible. This was mainly achieved by employing a part-time project manager, who had seemed sufficiently competent, motivated and capable of taking over from me, and who, more importantly, had the energy to meet the BWACS's mostly single-handed challenges and needs. I also saw to it that the newly appointed person not only enjoyed a good handover, but also a thorough induction.

On Monday 11th July 1994 I began work at Intentions, a position I settled into quite easily for apparent reasons. I was already familiar with the work in a way that Barbara wasn't, but I didn't pay too much attention to that; I just got on with things, happy to get stuck in and eager to prove to Barbara that she had done a good thing having faith and trust in me; for having made an investment in me in some way. In hindsight, I guess I set unconsciously about paying that investment off; an old familial pattern and haunt.

Overall, we all got along well. There was already some conflict between Barbara and the project's administrator, Mandy, who from the outset made it her duty to try and get me drawn into that conflict and on her side. She took great pleasure in informing me of Barbara's past relationships with previous employees. Mandy shared that although relationships between past employees and Barbara had started off well enough, and that Barbara at first had especially wanted them in particular to join the team, things had always gone on from there towards a bitter end. All of which had seen Barbara just as easily getting rid of those members of staff, and, according to Mandy, through off-handed measures.

Barbara and I had been getting along very well, and she hadn't been back-biting anyone, including Mandy, to me, so I concluded that for whatever personal reason, Mandy had it in for her and I should be careful not to get pulled in. It was an aspect of the job I felt disappointed about, especially with it coming so early into play, trying to rain on my parade. I so could have done without it.

I truly loved and enjoyed the work at Intentions, where I got better opportunities to do some good and deep hands-on counselling work with a regular, consistent and ongoing caseload. Intentions had so much potential and I was at its forefront, and I felt very honoured to be there. I contributed a tremendous amount to Intentions in regard to my work with clients, who tended to bond with me easily, becoming just as easily committed and motivated to understanding themselves, their situations and, very slowly but deliberately, considering and working towards change. Client work picked up significantly, and I was also able to make great contributions in the way of policies and clinical practice guidelines and procedures, and other relevant literature pertaining to related operational standards.

Ideas and information were just pouring out of me, and Barbara was happy to let me run with them. It wasn't long before she unofficially appointed me senior counsellor, which was the title I used when signing the various documents that I designed and created. I was so proud; I was very much Barbara's right-hand person, and she seemed very pleased with me, perhaps because I took my work very seriously, and she saw how it filled my heart to be doing really meaningful work with people in need. That's why it didn't faze me one little bit giving so much of myself and my ideas, as to my mind these vulnerable people, at the very least, deserved the best that we had to give.

Like already mentioned, Barbara and I got along just fine. As well as being happy to allow me to do my thing and express and share my ideas, she also used to lean on me for emotional support in regard to her personal life, which I didn't mind to begin with, but sometimes, especially with the out of office personal telephone calls, I did come to experience as burdensome. What felt particularly uncomfortable was the blurring of the employee-manager boundary, which brought back memories of how it used to be between Martha and me before all hell had broken loose.

Sometimes, it felt like I was more like the manager than Barbara. Sometimes it also felt like we were in danger of becoming more like friends rather than colleagues, which was slightly confusing. I would have preferred to have been left alone to do my job rather than sharing stuff that had nothing to do with work. Not that I didn't like or appreciate small talk; it just went on for way too long.

Within a couple of months of arriving at Intentions, I did pick up at times on Barbara's ambivalence towards me, and especially the position and prestige she had offered me as senior counsellor and how well I had filled it. It was as if every now and again she would kind of pull rank, covertly, but very definitely, letting me know who was indeed boss. She did this mostly during our supervision sessions, in which she was happy to 'educate' me, but like I had said, she had little to teach and offer, and seemed to be in greater need of being educated in the field herself.

I played along with her, but not too much, and not to the extent that she wanted. I couldn't willingly pretend not to know things; to me that seemed ludicrous and totally self-defeating. I began to feel that it would be in my best professional interest to find a way to play along with her, when I began to notice how frustrated and agitated she could become during our supervision sessions, even though she would try to hide it.

Instinctively, I knew that I needed to play this situation very carefully, especially when she kept on saying, and recording in supervision minutes, that I should use her and draw on her expertise in the field more. She tried to be sympathetic around my carrying my workload all on my own, when, like I said, all I could do was use her in the way that I could, as anything else would have been professional suicide.

I even began to think, at one time, that perhaps she was right. Due to past experiences, I knew that I had a tendency to think I was in it all on my own; that I couldn't depend on people and that I was some kind of superwoman. So, I tried to go along with her idea that I needed to allow her to support me more, but I still kept coming back and around to the fact that she, despite being my manager, was extremely inexperienced.

The behaviours that Barbara openly exhibited, and that left much to be desired and actively worked against her being an inspiration to me, or of being someone who had much to teach and was a good example to follow, were those related to the way in which she treated and behaved with and towards clients. She treated them almost as naughty little children who needed to be taught a lesson, especially when they didn't stop drinking and do as they were told to by her, the expert, during sessions.

Barbara was always more into solely focussing on clients' alcohol intake, and seemed to lack the very basic understanding, compassion and counselling skills that were also a very important part of the counselling process and work. She gave so much to them, or, more precisely, spent so much time trying to 'convince' them why they should stop drinking that sometimes her sessions went on for two or three hours. Then, when a particular client couldn't or wouldn't stop drinking immediately, she would chastise them when she saw them next, and so it went on. One time, she even stopped one of her most vulnerable and chaotic problem drinking clients from coming back to the centre until he did what she said and stopped.

Additionally, as project manager, Barbara wasn't even supposed to be doing much, if any, client work, but client work was what she seemed to prefer; it was where she loved to spend the better part of her working day. On top of all that, the organisation's approach to alcohol recovery was not based on the disease medical model of the likes of AA, but instead on social learning theory, and as such, on the idea that the client chooses which recovery path they would like to work towards: harminisation, control drinking or abstinence. The only time the client didn't have that choice was if they were wanting to get into one of the organisation's houses as part of a residential detoxification recovery programme, in which case abstinence would be the required option.

It began to become very clear to me that Barbara very much felt and saw Intentions as her baby and her brainchild, to do with as *she* liked. She was very much of the mind-set that she knew best, not only in regard to how Intentions as an organisation should operate, but also what the client needed. For both organisation and client, it was her way or the highway. I started to wonder how I could truly use this woman when she was totally off her trolley, a thing that became more and more apparent with the passing of each working day.

Barbara, at the best, or more precisely, at all times, was not open to suggestions or differences of opinions in any way, shape or form. She was extremely sensitive to criticism, constructive or otherwise. Through her own psychological makeup, she was well-defended; you just couldn't get through to her, so for the duration of the first six months' probation, I was now on red alert. I instinctively knew that I had to be careful; that I had to hold and keep certain things and perspectives back and to myself, at the very least until the probation period had passed, which would be in January 1995.

At around the same time as my probation period, I was still smoking weed, a thing that I also still desired to be rid of, and so I decided to look into getting me some therapy to help me give it up. I really wanted to get to the bottom of my weed smoking once and for all, and I especially wanted to seek out counselling in this regard because at times I felt like a hypocrite at work. I felt hypocritical and incongruent because I wasn't getting my own head enough around my own dependency on smoking weed, and it was important for me to be doing so, not only for my own recovery, but also in service of an inner satisfaction of knowing that I was being a better role model at my place of work.

I contacted and started therapy sessions at NAFYSIAT counselling service in Finsbury Park, North London, which was a culturally-specific counselling service developed to meet the needs of a diverse, multi-cultured society. On a donation-based, sliding scale fee scheme, NAFYSIAT provided weekly short-term therapy for anywhere between eight to twelve weeks, with the possibility of longer; the maximum amount of sessions being sixteen. At work, I had dressed it up as external supervision, which, as a personal development exercise, staff were allowed to pursue and take up, and Barbara was happy for me to leave work an hour earlier on a Fridays to access it.

The therapist I was assigned to work with was an art therapist, which was a bit different for me, having never experienced art therapy before. It involved talking about stuff, same as any other therapy, only while you are talking, you also paint as another form of unconscious communication and expression to be used to gain insight. And when the sessions, and discussions on my weed smoking, was truly under way, I began to realise just how many people around me smoked, whether it be friends or family.

All of my family members smoked weed at that time, including both my mother and father. From as far back as I can remember, smoking had been part and parcel of the scenery, which made me realise just how hard quitting would and had been. I hadn't truly acknowledged how pervasive it had been, and how on some deeper level, to me, weed smoking also meant fitting in. As I worked on these feelings, as well as other issues (e.g. the pain left over from the break up with Chris), I was still developing myself Afrocentric-wise, which also came to the surface during these sessions.

In the sessions, I took the time to address the African-Caribbean and black experience, which had felt like a really empowering thing to do, because even though the therapist wasn't black, (she was from another non-English speaking country), she was European and still very much white. I was still very much developing and understanding myself culturally, historically, spiritually and psychologically, and still very much reading the various literatures around these themes and perspectives. So, it felt quite liberating to feel comfortable enough to bring all these sides and developing parts of me into art therapy, and it felt equally good having it all accepted, respected, understood and acknowledged.

At the time of this bout of therapy, I was still continuing to make good progress in bringing healing to my inner and outer worlds, so much so that by the time 1995 came around, my dependency on weed began to dissipate, especially the 'need' for it. I was beginning to actually enjoy the periods of abstinence, which became more frequent and lasted for longer periods.

It was an abstinence that was still very much a work in progress at this time, but one that I patiently and deliberately continued to work towards, as somewhere inside I was determined to eventually make smoking weed a thing of the past. That was my ultimate goal, and because I had proven to myself that I could do it, mainly from the experience of having given up bulimia and so many and other equally difficult things since beginning on this journey, deep down I knew that given time, I could give up smoking weed, too.

BOOK THREE:

THE BITTER WITH
THE SWEET

CHAPTER FOUR

On 9th January 1995, I was to turn thirty years old. By way of celebration, the plan was to go to an R. Kelly concert with Sally and my sister Terri. The concert was great, and we really enjoyed ourselves. I wore this all-in-one black cat suit number, with knee-high nylon black boots and had the front part of my dreads up, cascading down in curls, as well as big hooped earrings and a short, waist-length black Bomber jacket. I looked and felt great.

After the concert, we were in Terri's car, going where I don't know; all I knew was that I wasn't ready to call it a night and go home, as I was too hyped up. Then, Terri shared that some of her work friends were having some kind of a party and suggested that we go there. When she said that, I had felt a little disappointed because I didn't fancy going to a work-type function to finish my birthday night off; I didn't even know her work friends. Anyway, during the ride she made a phone call to my sister Lauren, and when she came off the phone, she said that she had to go there quickly, just to pick something up, so off we went.

When we got to Lauren's, we all got out of the car, and Terri promised that we wouldn't be staying long. As we got to the main entrance, I noticed that the door was already open, and on the way up the stairs Terri asked if I could just run up and get whatever it was that Lauren had to give her, which I did. However, as I was making my way up the stairs, my mind was beginning to ponder, which it continued to do right up to the point that I opened up the living room door, and a room full of family and friends called out, 'Surprise!'

And boy, was it a surprise!

To think that they had arranged all this, a surprise thirtieth birthday party, Jamie included; Jamie, who I later learned had supplied the diary for numbers of friends without my knowledge, which in itself had surprised me. It really did turn out to be a great night; I didn't stop dancing until the party finished at 7am the next day. I received so much positive attention that night that it almost felt enough to have made up for all the attention I didn't get as a child. I felt cared for and cherished.

To top it all off, Michael had been roped in, which he was more than happy about. He was there to play the music; the good, sweet music that I loved. That's why I couldn't stop dancing; most of the night, non-stop, and with him, record after record. I was in heaven; it truly was a beautiful, most memorable night; one that in the years to come I would revisit and relish all over again in my mind, as well as through the many photographs that were taken. Only my sister Beverly was missing, as she was in South Africa with her new partner.

Later in the month, I passed my probation period at work with flying colours. All the hard work and tongue-biting had paid off, and Barbara was still very much happy with me overall. I received a glowing report in all areas, with the only negative, if you could even call it that, coming under the heading of 'Supervision.' Barbara still had those concerns; the ones pertaining to her fears that I wasn't using her as well as I could be, suggesting that there was still room for improvement and change in this regard, or words to those affects. It was as if Barbara wanted me to hold her in some particular kind of awe, and to worship the very ground she walked on -because she had made it possible for me to be at Intentions? Luckily for her, she was able to have a relationship of complete awe, control and domination with the newest member of staff, Frank. She had also influenced his coming into post.

Frank seemed to be totally taken in by her manipulations, and he was so totally grateful to her for pushing for him to get the job. Like me, he had also visited Intentions before, and expressed a similar desire to work somewhere similar, having been employed, again like me, as a sole worker alongside inexperienced, unreasonable and incompetent management committee members, providing specialist service provisions for the black community. Enter Barbara to the rescue, although not purely out of complete selflessness, as Frank, like me, had also been doing the job longer than she had, and thus had some good experience and expertise to bring to the table. You wouldn't believe that was the case judging by the way she treated him, though.

My first impression of Frank, when he first came on an outreach visit, was not a very good one. I found him, and his presence, quite irritating, and I had an immediate aversion to him. He seemed a bit pretentious in the way he was so nice and so in awe of Barbara; he just seemed somewhat smarmy with a touch of arrogance, despite trying to appear otherwise. Anyway, even though I was reluctant to truly see, accept or believe it, Barbara was beginning to feel extremely threatened by me.

Luckily, I was still in an Afrocentric state of mind, and as such I was still developing myself along those lines, especially spiritually, all of which gave me a kind of added faith, confidence, strength and very much a sense of 'back-up' during this time, as well as afterwards when things started to escalate. It was also during this time, May 1995, a month or so before the art therapy sessions came to an end, that Mark came into my life, mainly through the influence, or interference, of my sister Terri.

Terri had been going out with his friend Raymond at the time, and Mark had not too long come out of prison. I didn't know what for at the time, but much later down the line, as you do when you don't properly date and take the time to get to know someone, I found out that he had been in prison for selling weed. He had been in prison the best part of two years, but now he was out and had taken to linking back up with Raymond, oftentimes hanging out at Terri's house while waiting for Raymond to accompany him down the road, or just generally hanging out with him and Terri.

I don't know if Terri had thought that we would all make a nice foursome, or if she was basically just trying to get rid of him.

I'm not exactly sure what her motivations were, but she really did set about selling Mark to me, claiming how much alike we were based on all that he had shared with her. She described him as being positive, bright, determined, focused and forward-looking. I say 'claimed,' because as far back as I can remember, Terri has had a strong tendency to fabricate. As children, we used to call her 'Exaggerator the Great.'

Terri continued to play cupid, going on to tell me many more flattering things about Mark, and how she liked him and felt we would make a good pair; that we were well-suited. At first, I wasn't at all attracted to Mark. He was about six-foot, but while his body build was good enough, it had a kind of defeated look to it, and he had this kind of forbearance around him that worked against potential attractiveness. So, my initial feelings towards him were ambivalent, although I do remember the way in which I allowed myself to begin to change how I had initially felt, discounting instinct.

We were at Terri's house, the four of us, just chilling, and it was kind of alright. I remember staring him out, and in true 'Bluebird' style – that is, saying a thing is alright when your first impressions have already told you otherwise – trying to find something I could indeed find attractive about him and build on, which I eventually did with his eyes. In the foreboding energy surrounding him, there were these beautiful eyes. They were big and round, and ringed by these long, curled over lashes.

At the time, I didn't realise, as apparently these 'coming to be an item' kinds of things are more often than not arrived at subconsciously; my mother had arrived at a similar conclusion regarding my father and his gorgeous eyes. She had once shared that with me, or perhaps just said it out loud in general conversation. However, my mother and father hadn't gone on to become an item, she said he was too much of a womaniser.

Even after the 'at least he has nice eyes' Bluebeard conclusion, the kind that Clarrissa Pinkola Estes makes reference to in *Women who Run with the Wolves*, my ambivalence towards him still remained; one which saw me experiencing him, when he used to call, as something of a nuisance. Sometimes, I wouldn't even take his calls, asking Jamie to pass on my excuses of not being able to come to the phone, but when he persisted, I thought that maybe I should give him a chance. He did have those eyes, after all...

With work becoming quite difficult, and the loneliness of an unmet need for a consistent companion, I began to more seriously think that perhaps we could make a go of things. There were also the things Terri had said about him, especially him being like me; someone wanting change and to turn over a new, good leaf, and head towards a much improved and brighter future. If this was indeed the case, perhaps we would, I thought, turn out to be a match. This was a thought that came to excite me very much, and so I allowed myself to become more open to his advances, and to both him and us, the dream of *Happy Families* seeming to be possibility.

I had managed to cut down my weed smoking significantly, with which I was extremely pleased. However, having decided to give Mark and us a go, that recovery once again came to be on shaky ground, as Mark smoked religiously. I remember feeling vaguely disappointed by this, as I was still determined to eventually quit, and wasn't quite sure how I'd fair with such temptation at hand. At the time, I had thought that I would share with him what I was trying to achieve in regard to my smoking, but I didn't, rationalising that I could and would resist the temptation quietly, and not allow the situation to take me off course.

Like I said, I was a bit disappointed that he smoked, and to have found myself in the same situation that I had already half-resolved. I'd hoped that the next man I got involved with wouldn't do drugs, as I wanted the experience of having a relationship with a man who wasn't dependent on mood-altering substances.

In hindsight, things with Mark happened way too quickly from the get-go. We had only had one out of the house date – I still hadn't got the whole courting thing down to a tee – and I think things happened too quickly because he was manipulative and was pushing for it, with Terri oftentimes at work behind the scenes. One time, for example, she said that he had told her how much he had enjoyed spending an extended weekend at my house, so much so that he wasn't looking forward to going home and being away from me (wherever home was, as I wasn't quite sure and still struggled with believing that I had a right to ask questions about particular things). He had (supposedly) shared his enjoyment with Terri, and had been hoping that he could spend even more time with me going forward.

After the conversation, I was flattered that he'd felt that way and had shared his feelings so openly with Terri, but it also left me with a funny taste in my mouth, like I was being challenged to make his hopes and dreams of continued enjoyment come true, and rather underhandedly at that. I did enjoy his company, though, and he continued to present himself as Terri had testified. However, my uneasiness persisted, and I felt my suspicions were being confirmed when I noticed that directly after said conversation with Terri, he didn't even bother to go home when the weekend was well and truly over; like I said, wherever home was.

He immediately started staying over mine for longer and longer, without even asking or attempting to address the issue with me, putting me in a position where I had to bring it to him. This was a position that I generally hated and found most difficult, especially when I was already feeling so bamboozled, but I broached it with him anyway, endeavouring to do so in an open, honest, sensitive and caring way, bearing in mind all the things Terri had said he had said, and even surprising myself with my level of openness and assertiveness. In effect, I had concluded and shared that I wasn't ready to live with him yet, or indeed with anybody, without first taking enough time to get to know them and feel ready for that all-important next step. I had also shared some personal things about myself that I felt were related to the discussion.

Unfortunately, and rather surprisingly, it all fell on deaf ears, which I was a bit disappointed and amazed by. I say disappointed and amazed, because I felt that if he had really heard me, had really taken the time to listen and understand, and if indeed he was who he and Terri proclaimed him to be, that I wouldn't have got the reaction I did. The definite response was that what I had said was not what he had wanted, least of all expected, to have heard. In that moment, in true Bluebird colour and style, this situation very much foretold tell-tale signs of things to come;

things like how manipulative, controlling and domineering he could be.

It was like he completely ignored everything I had said, totally representing himself and going full force with what he absolutely wanted, which had been to move straight in. He pleaded his case by guilt tripping me with things like how he couldn't possibly leave me now, after spending so much time with me (all of two weeks!), how much he enjoyed my company and was really falling for me, how he'd be lost without me and so on and so forth. I could see how forceful and adamant he was about getting what he wanted, and getting me to see it solely from his (self-pitying) perspective. He was determined to change my mind and have me give him what he wanted. I could see how desperate he was to influence and persuade me, and to completely change my mind around to his way of thinking. I could see all this.

The situation was quite embarrassing really, and I was both dumbfounded and somewhat intimidated. He seemed so desperate, and I didn't feel like I had the bottle to persist with my perspective, even though he had given me enough reason to resist and lean more towards the bailing out of the relationship. Mixed in with all this, there continued the dance between Bluebeard and the yet to be fully wizened woman, demonstrated within a saving face, '*But then again...*'

But then again, I hadn't experienced this pleading in a relationship before; someone wanting to live and be with me so much as to be desperate. That thought took hold, and even though a part of me had clocked him and what he was and could be about, I caved. I gave in and instead, and at the very least, held him to being responsible towards the payment of certain bills, of which, and in apparent 'I've been successful' relief, he happily accepted and agreed to.

Like the once wounded and starved soul I had been, waiting, longing and yearning for someone – anyone – to commit and spend some time with me, in this regard, on this level, Mark had been available and reliable. Unlike Ronald and past parental figures, he didn't go out much, and as such seemed more than happy to be around. So, I told myself that this man really liked me and loved being with me, but the bitter taste remained somewhere. I wasn't that out of my head. I had already come way too far to be that far gone.

Later that day, after being manipulated into us living together, I returned home to find that he had cooked dinner. No sooner had I taken off my shoes and put my slippers on than he'd brought me in a plate of food, consisting of Ackee and salt fish with dumpling, sweet potatoes and plantain, and like a good little puppy, I ate it all up. When I was done, he followed it with a ready-made spliff, all of which I had appreciated, and all of which had worked its magic, if that's what had been intended.

Not too long after Mark moved in, two months later to be exact, I unintentionally became pregnant, following a major mess-up with the contraception pill. I had been taking contraception pills that were too strong and had been taken off the market, unbeknownst to myself until I went to get some more at the local family planning clinic and was informed as such. Naturally, I stopped taking them, and in the interim before starting a new and updated brand, I became pregnant.

At that time, Barbara and I had managed somehow to sort out our differences, so much so that when a deputy manager position came up, she went out of her way to encourage me to apply, going so far as to imply that the job was already mine. I believed her, since I was already doing the job unofficially, and it suited my professional development prospects to get the actual title, promotion and recognition. Barbara had also given me the impression that all I had to do was fill in the application form and go through the motions of an interview. According to her, that would be all there was to it, as she had already put in a very good word for me.

I was experiencing major internal conflict after becoming pregnant and previously thinking, before the promotion interception, that perhaps I would keep it. However, I now found myself leaning more towards the job, not only because I out and out wanted the promotion, but also due to the growing realisation of the fact that the pregnancy had come too soon. Another issue was that when I had found out I was pregnant and shared the news with Mark, he'd been very happy and we'd both agreed to go through with it. So, I was in quite a dilemma, although not for too long, because I soon made up my mind and decided not to go through with the pregnancy, to Mark's utter disgust and dismay.

Mark was bitterly disappointed and angry, but these were feelings that I tolerated and essentially put up with because I empathised. I could understand his anger over feeling left out when I made the final decision, essentially on my own. I didn't talk too long about it with him, because intuitively, and from past experience, I knew he would try and talk me out of it; something he did go on to try and do, even, and once again, getting Terri on side. It's also possible that I put up with his totally free expression of ill feeling towards me because, deep down, I felt I deserved it for making the decision to terminate a budding life.

Regardless, given the circumstances at the time, the decision had 'felt' right, and I was prepared to face up to and to live with the consequences of my actions. Like I said, Mark was far from happy, and he never tried to understand or come around to my way of thinking. Instead, he went right out of his way to let me know, at any given time, exactly what he thought and felt, holding absolutely nothing back. His lamentations picked up further speed on the actual day of the termination and upon my return from the private hospital post-termination..

That day, it had been particularly hot, and he, immediately upon my arrival home, had been so cold, uncaring and unsympathetic, cursing me out and saying the most horrible, guilt-inducing things he could think of. He told me what a cold-hearted, murdering bitch I was, and how I should feel guilty for killing an innocent baby; things one feels already in such circumstances without having to hear it, and especially in that way. It was awful.

He became nastier and more aggressive with each passing day, holding me hostage night after night to his feelings and mood swings; to his ranting, ravings and blaming. One night, after he had had some kind of bust up with his mum, who was visiting from Jamaica at the time, he came home in a crazy mood, claiming he very nearly ended his life by jumping off some building, which he blamed on my decision to terminate. He had scared the shit out of me that night, so much so that I truly began to wonder what the hell I had gotten myself into.

I feared for my safety, and felt terrible feelings of powerlessness. I had no choice but to listen to him, keeping my mouth shut right up and paying attention, lest I get terribly wounded. I could feel the bait; it was like he wanted me to lose my cool and to react, in his eyes, unfavourably, just so he had a good enough reason to physically do me something.

Night after night, for weeks after the termination, he kept me up with his ranting and ravings, way into the early hours of the morning, knowing full well I had to go to work. It must have given him some kind of powerful feeling, him seeming to have such power and control, and completely intimidating me. Truly, it was like he was having some kind of psychotic breakdown. Finally, to make matters worse, I didn't even get the job. Barbara had gotten it so totally wrong, and in so doing, especially as manager, not encouraged me to prepare myself sufficiently to make getting the job a definite reality. I felt such a fool!

The interview was a complete surprise, as well as an embarrassment, for the precise reason of my not being fully prepared. The managers were expecting a detailed presentation with charts and everything, which had been news to me! I ended up feeling quite emotional and humiliated in my unpreparedness, and when I came back from the interview and shared the whole experience with Barbara, she burst into tears, which had thrown me. She seemed just as upset, maybe even more so, if that was at all possible. Perhaps at that point she realised the part she had played in it, and how much I had sacrificed to get the job she had promised was mine already (she had known about the termination).

Whatever the case, she bawled like a baby, and I ended up attempting to console her when it was me that was in desperate need of consoling. After that, she immediately tried to rectify the situation by arranging a meeting with the same senior managers that had interviewed me, but it was to no avail and the decision stood. It was out of her hands, not that it ever was in her hands, as she herself had arrogantly and mistakenly believed.

The whole situation had made me wonder if, in addition to everything else, the managers were, through me, teaching Barbara a lesson. She had a horrid reputation with senior management, who were very familiar with her shortcomings and wrongdoings. Whatever the case, it was a truly awful ordeal, during a period that was a general low point in my life. In her apparent guilt, Barbara suggested, and I happily accepted, that I take two weeks off for 'study leave,' which was another one of her very many inventions.

BOOK THREE:

THE BITTER WITH THE SWEET

CHAPTER FIVE

Study leave could have been even more beneficial to me if I'd had the chance to make full use of it, but alas, Mark was there to spoil it, or at least the whole of the first week. When he eventually calmed himself down, or wore himself, and my last nerve, out, he apologised and promised to take better hold of himself, saying that surely, I could understand where he was coming from. Then it wasn't too long before he was off on another tantrum. This time, the tangent was brought on by the difficulties he was experiencing finding work. Not that he had shared this, but I somehow deduced it after another one of those 'advocate Terri' calls.

This time, she shared with me how he had shared with her how tempting it was for him to go back to selling weed, a thing that had landed him in prison in the first place, and a thing her partner, Mark's friend, juggled himself. During a conversation that Mark and I went on to have, coincidently following the conversation with Terri, I couldn't help but feel that he, like her, was rather underhandedly feeling me out and gauging my thoughts regarding him getting back into weed selling. During the conversation, he had said to me how an old friend of his had said that he should consider it, reminding him how good he had been at peddling it, and how he easily kept and maintained a regular and consistent client base; words to that effect.

Like I said, the conversation felt very manipulative and indirect to me, to which I directly and clearly responded by reminding him of his goals, plans and dreams, as well as the reason he was imprisoned in the first place. By the way he behaved for a time after this, I don't think that disapproval was actually what he wanted to hear from me. I think he just had assumed that I would have been one of those women who didn't mind how he brought in the bacon, so long as he did.

Anyway, after a little while he pulled himself out of his sulk, and instead became even more helpful around the house, cooking, cleaning and mending things, etc. However, this was a house that I wished he would sometimes leave, at least long enough so that I could get some good quality time alone. I was getting fed up of coming home from work and wishing that he would be out, and then finding him as per usual plonked in front of the television; it really did begin to get on my nerves. However, when he was on his best behaviour, he could be very attentive, as well as gentle, kind and loving, and it was essentially for these reasons that I stayed with him.

Those were the things that I loved about him, and made me love him enough to think that hope still existed; that made me think that I should be a little bit more patient, and that as a couple we really had potential. I knew that he would be the kind of man that would marry me, and like I said before, I had never previously been in a relationship with someone who doted on me and was so domesticated, as well as attentive when he put his mind to it. Jamie also got along well-enough with Mark, be it more from a distance- and vice-versa. I had thought at the time that it would be good for Jamie to see a man around the house taking on household tasks.

Still, there was no denying that it was like he was two people inside, and one of them was filled with rage, which made me terribly afraid of him, and perhaps afraid of leaving him, too. So, I bided my time, both with Mark at home and Barbara at work. The latter was back up on one of her power trips again, but luckily I was already on the journey, and in so being and doing, I had a growing confidence, faith, strength and spiritual life, all of which kept me hopeful and determined inside.

At the time, I also used to keep a 'Black Pearls' journal, which I would write in before retiring most evenings. It was a journal within which I would either use its opening entry of a particular positive affirmation as a starting point for my own thoughts on a subject, as it pertained to my experience of life, or come up with starting points of my own, usually related to how badly Barbara or Mark had behaved towards me that day. Basically, I was still using my love of creative writing to turn ill feelings back around, making all grist for the never ending self-development mill.

I was determined not to let Mark, Barbara or indeed anything else get the better of me, and least of all to deter me from the good things that I believed were lying in wait for me, somewhere. I had also been reading, studying, and particularly enjoying the *Metu Neter* volumes one and two, a spiritual cultivation text based on ancient Egyptian practises, vision and wisdom. So, even though there was a lot going on, inside I felt strong, and there continued to be this inner knowing that things would come to pass, and that, however dark it all seemed, all was indeed still very well. Physically, emotionally, and mentally I sometimes would feel worn out by it all, of which, and then, on my own, I would cry. Despite this, I always woke in the morning feeling strengthened and refocused, and so I went on.

At work, the struggle continued and saw Barbara working even more feverishly on the mission: 'Get Marcia on Disciplinary Action.' Everywhere and anywhere, there she was, trying hard to find fault, and now she had Frank at her side, her faithful steed, whom she had trained to worship and represent her, especially in her absence. It was a combination of everything, especially the situation at work, that had brought to mind a certain idea that I proceeded to share with Mark, which I guess suggests that my mind was already made up.

The idea was the thought of having a child. Like I said, Mark had calmed down somewhat, and we seemed to be getting along fairly well, and what with work being the way it was, having a child at that time began to seem like a very good idea. The idea also, more at the back of my mind, presented itself as a temporary way out; not that I liked thinking of it in that way. I still very much loved my job in terms of the actual work, but I needed some kind of respite through which I could come to see a much better way forward.

Additionally, the decision to have a child was also very much based on the fact that I was already in a relationship and, I had thought, that I wasn't getting any younger. In my heart of hearts, I had hoped that I would have been settled by now with a couple more children, to say the least. There had been a very strong feeling that in the childbearing department, time was running out. I was now thirty-one. Of course, there also existed the fact of the previous termination, which perhaps I was trying to assuage guilt over and make right. Then, there was Mark, who in spite of himself also wanted a child, which got me to thinking that just like the experience of having Jamie had done for me, given me good and just cause to turn my world around, that perhaps our child could do the same for him.

From the beginning of the relationship, Mark had shared his awful childhood with me. The abuse sounded really awful and relentless, and had continued right up until Mark was fifteen years old and couldn't take it anymore. At the time, he had truly believed and thought that his father would kill him, or that he would kill his father in self-defence and piled upon unexpressed rage.

Needless to say, Mark was happy with the idea of having a child, and resolved to try even harder to be a better person; to get his life in a certain order. So, we became pregnant, but the conflict at work, quite disappointingly, heightened, rather than dissipated as I'd expected, due to them 'knowing my condition.' I think Barbara was trying to make it really hard for me, especially now that I was pregnant. She wanted to drive me out and make me quit from the sheer exhaustion of it, and it was exhausting! Little did she know how many people I had to keep stopping from coming to my place of work to do her something, both Mark and my sister Terri included.

Sadly, and before long, Mark flipped again. It truly seemed that he had something inside him that made it nearly impossible for him to be happy for long, which was also disappointing, because it now looked and seemed that not even the dream, be it mines or his, of us making and being a happy family, was enough to keep him on an even keel.

It began to be clear that the side of him that was more bullying, aggressive, manipulating, controlling, hurt and in total rage and pain was much stronger and real than the other side of him, because no matter what, that rage-filled bullying side just kept returning. Eventually, he came to be, like Barbara, totally unsympathetic and indifferent to my being pregnant. The fact that I was carrying his child made absolutely no difference, as he slipped totally back into attack mode, endeavouring to assert terror and control. I didn't even know what kicked it off, all of which gave me grave concerns about his ability to be a dad, especially the kind of father a child needs, the one thing that there could be no compromising on for me.

This realisations and the ongoing situation of Mark's changing moods and volatility, gave me the something I finally needed to set about ending the relationship with Mark. There was no way I was going to let myself, and any child of mine, be subject to that kind of behaviour. Mark had way too many issues. So one day

I planned my escape, knowing that the time had come to make that move. Somehow, I intuitively knew that I was ready, and I also knew just how to go about it. It was like some other kind of inner being was now in charge of things, an energy and presence I had oftentimes felt during the most testing periods of my life. It was time to act.

As in the case of domestic violence, and all other types of abusive behaviours, Mark had hidden his bad behaviour behind closed doors and outside of witnesses. In regard to Jamie, Mark behaved badly when he was out with friends or in bed asleep. Jamie was thirteen at the time and used to play a lot of football, but I'm sure he must have heard and picked up on things anyway. I always tried extra hard to 'behave myself,' (i.e. keep quiet and out of his way) whenever Jamie was home and Mark's temper was brewing.

On the day I had planned to make my departure, I had told Jamie not to go home but to go straight from school to meet me at the bus stop. It was a Friday, and after we met at the bus stop, we took the bus straight to my sister Terri's house. I knew that I needed that kind of backup, just like I had known it when I was breaking up with Michael, and my sister Beverly had then been chosen to act in that particular vein.

I told Terri everything, who was very shocked to say the least, as well as somewhat disbelieving, since the Mark I was describing was not the Mark she thought she knew; the one she had introduced to me. Yet, in her apparent disbelief, she tried to be understanding and supportive of me, and later in the evening, from her house, I called Mark on the phone and requested that he leave. I could hear how shocked he was, and I even put Terri on the phone to have some kind of word with him. I think he was in shock mainly due to the fact that I had brought Terri into it; that I had played that particular hand.

I spent the night at Terri's, to ensure that he got the message and would be gone by the time of my return the next day, which he was, but he didn't leave the keys as I'd requested. Later that day, he used those keys to let himself in and immediately set about giving me a piece of his mind, before finally throwing the keys at me hard on his way out.

I was very disappointed that my carrying his baby hadn't been enough for him to change his ways. I was also disappointed with the prospect of being pregnant and alone – even though I was prepared to go it alone. All this hurt some place deep in my core. This was so not what I had imagined when I had imagined bringing another child into the world. I had wanted the total package, including marriage.

Back at work, Barbara had finally succeeded in getting me on a disciplinary, issuing me with a three-month verbal warning. I was six months pregnant by then, and her unfounded grounds for disciplinary action were that she felt and believed, and attempted to prove, that I hadn't been working well, if at all, with alcohol units within my work with clients, implying that perhaps I didn't know how, and needed some further development and training. Barbara stooped as unscrupulously low as to misuse the fact that one of my clients had died to mount her case against me, and give her story some sort of credibility.

I was so disappointed and enraged with her and her level of

vindictiveness. She knew full well that I knew how to do my work in this area, and that the accusation of my not being able to was indeed pure fabrication, for it had never been an area of concern during the probation period and the final successful completion of it. All it was really about was the fact that she and I worked differently.

Yes, that particular client had died, and in actual fact we never came to know the exact reason why. Yes, he knew he was diabetic, and through our work together also came to know how detrimental continuing to drink could be to this health, yet still he chose to continue, and I was there for him regardless, as should always be the case. You can't force people into making certain decisions if they don't want or feel able to do it. In the sessions we had been working with all that and more, so I was incredibly incensed at Barbara's accusations!

To top it all off, the real professional misconduct regarding that particular situation came as a result of the fact that when he had died, Barbara hadn't even thought to support me as my so-called manager and clinical supervisor. Instead, here she was choosing to use his passing to mount a case against me; to use his death to further her own crazy needs and ends. This, in turn, made me crazy, especially because I had done some really promising work with the client in question, from which he had clearly benefited, so much so that hearing of his passing had truly impacted me. The client himself would be turning in his grave at what Barbara was suggesting!

At that time, I truly began to see the truth in Mandy's words, especially what she had said about how dirty Barbara's fighting could be; how low she would, could and did go, and the delight she took in having people fear her. That's how she had told Mandy she preferred to rule, to get respect and her dues.

Anyway, to my utter disgust, surprise and dismay, Barbara was able to get away with it. I believe she was able to do this firstly because I wasn't represented well, as it was my first time being in such a predicament, so didn't know how to act in a way to better represent myself, and secondly due to the incompetence of a senior manager, who had heard the case and wasn't even really at all interested in getting involved. It was like he just wanted it over and done with.

In actual fact, after I had appealed the decision, and he had gone on to still rule in her favour, he promptly left the organisation amidst rumours of some kind of senior management restructuring and ongoing workplace conflict. Even Barbara was surprised when he finally ruled in her favour, I saw it in her face; that's how shallow and see-through she was. I could see that she was surprised by the news that she had gotten away with it, so much so that even though she didn't like the man – she had told us this on a number of occasions – she sent him a farewell card. Now she had finally found a leg to stand on; finally found something to hold over me and try to take back some kind of power, control and authority, she feared she had lost to me, whilst in the process of trying to make my life a misery. .

There were also the Mandy effects, which were adding into the mix more than their two pennies' worth. Mandy, who couldn't hide her 'told you so' delight at the way things were panning out. I hadn't thought that things could have got much worse than they had in the days of Martha and Chris, but this situation far outweighed both that and anything else I could remember having been through.

Perhaps it was no wonder, with everything that had been going on, that I had suffered through the first four months of pregnancy with terrible morning, afternoon and evening sickness. I'd had morning sickness with Jamie, but nowhere near as badly, and I'm certain that those very stressful situations didn't help. The sickness got so tiresome that it had become a great relief to get home and, once I had got the various things that had to be taken care of after work out of the way, to escape straight into sleep. I was in bed by 9.30pm most evenings.

The sickness even made work, that is escaping into it, a saving grace, as being there and being thusly occupied gave me less time to focus on feeling sick. However, I was able to, on the whole, enjoy most of my pregnancy, even after the sickness and need to spit went away, and was for the duration then replaced with general on and off heartburn. I was also able to finally give up smoking weed when I became pregnant!

Regarding the disappointment of having to go it alone as a parent again, I tried not to have any regrets. I didn't wish that I wasn't pregnant, and I still wanted to be, but I knew I had some work to do in order to come to terms with it; to deal with how it had all turned out. So, it wasn't long before I got myself into some short-term therapy with this man I met through work, Nelson Philips.

Nelson Philips had provided Intentions with workshops, training events and the likes, the most recent event being on the subject of better dealing with in-house conflicts in the workplace. I respected Nelson; he was professional, and he had a good understanding, working knowledge and involvement with Afrocentricity, mental health and well-being. Also, he was both a psychotherapist and a black man, and I had never experienced receiving therapy from a black man before, so I had thought it would be an altogether good experience.

To cut a long story short, I worked with him, as before, under the guise of personal development during work hours, as he practised just up the road from Intentions. I worked with Nelson for two and a half months, right up until the time I took maternity leave in June 1996, during which he not only helped me come to terms with the Mark pregnancy situation, but also supported me in regard to Barbara and the ongoing conflicts at work. He hadn't realised, although he had suspected, how off her head Barbara indeed was, and it felt good to have that thought confirmed and a part of myself reassured. It was a part of me that, at times, in all the Mark, Barbara and earlier devastating life experiences and situations, had left me despairingly wondering, *Why do all these crazy things keep happening to me? Is it me?*

The work with Nelson also reassured fears I had concerning the prospects of my unborn child faring with such a damaged and wounded father, and whether it would affect his or her biological make up. Nelson was able to reassure me that while sometimes it could be argued that the apple doesn't fall too far from the tree, in other circumstances that needn't be and oftentimes is not the case.

At the time, I had needed to see, hear and know these things, and had come to an important realisation in the midst of it: *Look at me! Look at me!* I myself had fallen some way away from the tree, and as my spiritual friends have, on important occasions, reminded me, all most definitely was not lost and forgotten with me! *So*, I decided, *this shall be the case with my baby.*

Back to Love

BOOK FOUR:

SECONDS IN, TIME-OUT

CHAPTER ONE

**"God can heal a broken heart,
but she has to have all the pieces"**

I enjoyed being pregnant again, just like I had when I was carrying Jamie. Mark and I were still very much over, and he had fled to Jamaica to spend time – six months, to be exact – with his parents, so I hadn't seen him from the time we'd broke up right through the duration of my pregnancy. I was still very angry at him for the way he had treated me, and overall very disappointed at how things had all turned out yet again. Sometimes, I even felt a bit embarrassed being a single parent and so completely on my own, right from the word go. Sadly, that reality did detract somewhat from the experience, I must admit.

I had truly hoped that at this juncture in my life, I would have been much better at relationships, especially the male-female variety, particularly after spending three years celibate, and then being alone again after the Chris experience. But here I still was, getting relationships terribly and utterly wrong. I was at a loss, and almost on the verge of entirely giving up in regard to that area of my life, yet still I was thankful to have my soon-to-be-born baby to keep me company, along with Jamie.

I was also very thankful to be off work; so very glad, in fact, as it had been so stressful, and not particularly because I was pregnant, although that obviously played a part in, but mostly because Barbara really had turned the heat right up. She felt no compassion for the fact that I was carrying a child; she really disappointed me. She disappointed me in regard to the fact that she could have been so bitter and twisted, not only as a fellow human being, but also as a woman, and a woman who knows what it's like to be with child; she was a mother herself. So, I was happy that work was just a distant memory for the time being, and glad to be rid of the stress and demands it brought. The responsibility of taking Jamie to football matches, both home and away, as well as the various other football events continued for a while, as he had no one else, but when I got to eight months I had to ease off it quite a bit, as everything was beginning to feel too much.

During the last two weeks of my pregnancy, I had allowed Jamie to go with his football club to America for a week in order to take part in a tournament. It was the first time we had been separated for a whole week, and at that kind of a distance it was a big thing for me to allow. I myself had not travelled by then (and still haven't to date, due to fears of flying), but I knew that I had to let him go because it would be a good experience for him, as well as for me, and the rest of the team were going, although most of them were to be accompanied by at least one of their parent.

It was a challenge getting the money together. I got a bit from his dad, but I had to provide the bulk of it via scrimping and saving and a bank overdraft, but I just about scraped up enough for him to have spending money. Anyway, he went, and whenever we spoke on the phone, he seemed to be having a great time, which made me happy; happy especially to have been able to allow him to go.

It wasn't long after Jamie had returned home safely that I went into labour, an experience that, this time around, I coped very well with. With Jamie, it had been an extremely painful labour that had started with broken waters the day before, but then no contractions, which led to the decision to induce me early the next morning. His birth had been hard, which had resulted in me tearing quite a bit and loosing quite a bit of blood. The pain had been quite intense, so much so that I remember seriously wishing at one point that I hadn't become pregnant; that I could somehow turn the clocks back.

With this pregnancy, it was different. Obviously, it wasn't my first, so I knew, to a certain extent at least, what to expect, and I was a lot more relaxed and prepared. This time, I only used gas and air, whereas with Jamie I'd had one or two pain-numbing and relieving injections. With this delivery, I worked much better with the contractions, and like I said, with just the gas and air, only having to push a couple of times, whereupon my baby arrived at the beginning of the third push. No tearing, no loss of blood;

just a beautiful baby boy, weighing in at 6lbs 13oz at 6.56am on August 13th 1996, to very proud and happy mummy.

On the whole I was happy with my baby and with the delivery experience, but the thing that was difficult, that I only became aware of the night after the first visit from family and friends, was the absence of spouse; at least Ronald had been there with Jamie. This absence of spouse became so painfully obvious that particular evening, and during the days and evenings that followed, as visitors left and partners of the other mums on the ward remained.

Not that I was the only single parent; there was also a young girl who was in the bed besides me, but I truly felt the isolation, loneliness, abandonment, disappointment and pain, as well as the yearning for it not to have been this way; for it to have been different. Like I said, not having the father to share in the experience took something away from it for me, as second time around that had definitely been the hope and dream.

Life went on, though, as it always has to, and in spite of it all, the joy far outweighed the pain and disappointment, especially the joy that comes with being a more experienced and emotionally mature second time mum, notwithstanding the total experience of being off work.

The only other troubling situation that I had to contend with was money matters. Money had become very tight again, especially since I'd had to find the funds needed to allow Jamie the football holiday experience, in addition to being a totally single parent, solely responsible for all that was needed. The situation became even more challenging when my salary went from full to half pay, and then to no pay at all for the final three months of my leave, when I had to go on benefits because I had chosen to take the full year maternity leave option. Financially, it felt so bad at the time, so much so that I took out a loan.

Early during the week of my returning home with baby Julian, Terri twisted my arm, or at least that's what it felt like, once again, although it wasn't so clear to me at the time, into agreeing to let Mark come and visit Julian, as he had been back in the country a couple of weeks. This conversation had taken place on the actual drive home from the hospital, after she picked me up and dropped me off, being as she was the only one in the family who was driving at the time.

During the conversation, I ended up feeling bad and guilty for not really wanting to allow Mark access; guilt mixed in with a bit of unentitled anger at Terri for seeming to forget the way he had treated me, and also and obviously anger at Mark for how he had gone completely missing during the pregnancy, only to now want to see the baby and play Happy Families.

I was pissed off, but I gave in because the guilt felt stronger, especially the guilt that came in the way she had pleaded his case and left me feeling that I was being the unreasonable one, insinuating that what was between him and me was nothing to do with the baby. Deep down, however, I was not happy, and it was so incredibly hard allowing him to be around; to have him back in my house and near my new-born child.

When he came that first time, teddy bear in hand, I wanted to rip his heart out; to let him know what he had done and how it had felt. I really felt like I wanted to throw up. I couldn't bare being in his presence, and especially not in my own house. As the days went by, I continued to allow him to see Julian here and there, especially as I had also picked up on Terri's and my mother' vibes that suggested that a man should be allowed to be in his child's life, irrespective of how he behaves.

So, I went along with it, all the while feeling confused, resentful and betrayed, especially at all the pretence, and perhaps angry at myself for what felt like, and in effect was, totally compromising myself.

Anyway, Mark came, asking what was needed, bringing a pushchair and other bits and pieces, which didn't take away from how I was truly feeling; it all seemed to make no difference to me. Also, surprise, surprise, his good behaviour didn't last for long – about two weeks in all. He soon fell back into his aggressive, dominating and controlling ways when he couldn't have exactly what he wanted, as and when he wanted it, like attending more often, uninvited, which saw him becoming threatening and all the rest, leaving me no choice but to cancel the ill-advised arrangement. He reacted by breaking off all assistance in the way of financial contributions, making it clear that it was his way or no way.

Before long we got into an on again-off again pattern, this time in the relationship between him and Julian, which saw him, as per usual, going through Terri to get his renewed promises and sorry-arse messages across to me. The compulsion to repeat pattern occurred three times in all, and every time it ended the same way and every time the bad behaviour came to pass, I was able to draw from the experience added conviction and strength regarding the validity and truth embedded within my first decision that he could not have much to do with Julian, as he just wasn't up to it. He was just so totally unable to be the kind of father that Julian needed.

The three failed attempts at establishing a secure the father-child bond occurred when Julian was one and a half, three, and 8 years old, but it was the second and third attempts that made me draw a line under forcing this father-son fit…

When Julian was three years old I allowed Mark to take Julian to see his mother, who was visiting from Jamaica and staying at his brother's house, as she and her husband had gone back home to Jamaica to live some years prior. She hadn't seen Julian before, and upon their return, Julian was being a bit grizzly because he was tired after what had been a long day for him. However, his behaviour wasn't anything untoward or out of hand, as generally he was by nature a calm, happy and easy-going child.

Mark, rather disturbingly, responded to his tiredness and moaning by promptly hitting him hard over the head with an empty shoe box that had been resting close by on the sofa. Julian, never having been lashed out at like that before, looked at Mark in absolute shock and horror, and started to cry really hard, whereupon Mark, realising what he had done, collected himself and attempted to console him, which Julian just was not interested in receiving, least of all from the person who had just hurt him.

After witnessing that scene, I knew that Mark, however hard he tried, would end up bringing Julian more pain than joy and doing him more harm than good. I knew in that instant that Mark himself needed professional help if he was ever going to offer a semblance of the kind of parenting that not only Julian needed, but he himself, in his right mind, would also wish to give. I knew that Mark wouldn't be able to work this out himself, and in the interim, there was no way I was going to let Julian be anybody's guinea pig, his father included.

When I tried to address the situation with Mark, also suggesting he go get counselling to help him with his anger, as usual, he was not open to it. He was not open to what I was saying, and instead he turned it all back onto me, arguing that there was no situation, and that it was just me trouble-making and being difficult because I couldn't get my own way; because I wanted to be in complete control and have total charge of things; just me trying to make mountains out of molehills. So, there was another parting of ways, as again he dropped completely out of the picture, which also meant the total withdrawal of financial support.

The third and final attempt took place in the summer of 2004. Mark had not too long come out of prison and had made contact. He had been serving two years in prison for the same reason as before, just what I had predicted and had feared would happen if things with Mark didn't change; the thing that had been one of the main reasons, outside of his rage, why I didn't want Julian being exposed to his world. What with all the (drug related) black on black gun crime developing at that time, there was no way I was going to allow Julian to be party to those particular kinds of outcome.

Whilst in prison Mark had shared that he had been doing some college courses and was determined to sort out some kind of employment for himself, when he came out, but it wasn't long before he went straight back into peddling dope. Even though he had had some kind of counselling in prison, it also wasn't before too long that his temper came a-knocking, banging down the door. His bad behaviour came out when I had clearly, and in no uncertain terms, stipulated that I didn't want him smoking dope or drinking alcohol before or during the two hours of father-son time he spent out with Julian, an arrangement I allowed, and stipulations he disregarded.

Mark always thought that I was making a great big deal out of nothing; out of his environment; out of his dealing and smoking weed; out of his rages and out of his alcohol consumption. He felt I was making much more of a big deal of all these things compared to the other women he had known and was more used to dating. Having grown up in a similar kind of environment of weed dealing, smoking, drinking and hustling, I was more than fully aware of its apparent dangers, especially toward the ruined innocence of children, forcing them to grow up way before time.

It was during this last ditch attempt that I was finally able to see and accept the fact that Mark, through his own limitations and needs, just could not give Julian, let alone himself, what he needed. It had taken this long for me to know that it's OK for me to see and acknowledge that, and to do what I had to do to better protect my son. Besides, Julian didn't really know his dad. There was no bond, even though I had endeavoured to have them create one through these (unrealistic) attempts, , I noted that Julian felt at a loss as to how to be or what to do in the presence of his father, and Mark was no different towards him. Julian was eight years old at the time.

In the midst of finally accepting Mark's apparent limitations, there was also the bittersweet disappointment and concerns about a child, especially a son, not growing and coming to know his dad and being positively influenced by him. Like I said previously, it mattered to me especially because that was also my story, so some of my own psychological wounds and grief processes resurfaced. The sadness and disappointment also came about due to a mother, me, wanting the best for her child, especially her black male child living in, among other things, a racism-riddled society. Even though Ronald had fallen short in certain areas, Jamie at least *knew* his dad; they had, when it mattered most, enjoyed a father-son bond, and continued to have a relationship.

I reconciled myself to the observable reality that Julian was a very happy, confident, secure and well-rounded child; that he had the best of me and of possible starts, which perhaps was enough. I had to release his dad; to let that particular unfulfilled dream go, and relate more consciously to the reality of the situation.

During this time I also had to take Terri to task, which had been a long time coming! Over the years, her loyalty towards and alliance with Mark had remained, which was something that I just could not understand, what with her being my sister and all. When I finally took her in hand, she just couldn't see how destructive her speaking and acting on his behalf was to our own relationship, nor her misguided thoughts about Mark being allowed to still have a relationship with Julian.

Being as wrong and strong as she could be, Terri just couldn't see or understand where I was coming from, almost seeing me, like Mark had, as the bad guy, all of which was terribly upsetting, not least because she is my sister, but because I had told her how Mark was and what he done to me. However, she wouldn't have it; she just couldn't get it. She just couldn't get anything that hinted at her being wrong.

So the breaking point came, and I just had to let her have it. I just had to tell her, and in no uncertain terms, to keep her nose out of my business. She had never seen me get angry with her like that before, if at all, and consequently, I heard through the family grapevine that in her own upset, she had gone on to say some not very nice things about me. However, regardless of what she said about me, as long as she had got the message, I was happy. With a line now drawn under her interference, my job had been done.

As is usually the case throughout trials and tribulations, what continued to keep me confident, faithful and strong was this growing spirit and inner belief in myself, and of all things of and for me. Just before Julian had been born, I had set up a spiritual development alter in a corner of my bedroom, which I still have to this day. I was reading a lot of Iyanla Vanzant at the time, and had gotten the idea of a spiritual development alter from her book, *Tapping the Power Within*.

I was also still not smoking weed, and I knew that I would never smoke it again. What finally sealed it for me was an experience I had after having Julian. It was the same week that I brought him home, and someone had left me a spliff. I had attempted to smoke it, but then I immediately didn't like the way that it began to make me feel. That feeling had frightened me. The experience scared me because it felt and seemed that it could harm and get in the way of, and work against, the crucial bond being gingerly developed between Julian and myself.

I had feared that smoking weed would have an overall negative influence and impair that *critical and scared* bonding period in the weeks following birth, and I so wanted to truly take the opportunity to start this mother-child experience and journey totally free and independent of weed. Not that I had smoked weed when Jamie was a very young child; my regular weed smoking begun to take root when he was around four or five years old.

I had felt quite proud of myself for coming to the decision to never go back to weed smoking; to coping with life in that way. Proud of myself and overjoyed someplace important inside, because I knew that I had finally triumphed and was no longer clouding my heart, soul and mind with dope. Having smoked weed for ten years and then being completely without it during my pregnancy, all manner of things appeared more clearly to me, and helped me to truly see and feel its negative effects and influences.

There was no denying that not smoking weed was a totally different experience than smoking it, but one you could only come to know from the experience of being free of it for a significant period of time. Smoking and giving up smoking weed for me had been like not needing, but still wearing, bifocals, and then taking them off and finally being able to see things as they truly were. I guess it's not called 'dope' for nothing.

There were other changes that I made at the time, like starting Julian on a healthy and wholesome homemade vegetarian diet, a path that I was already on, and had Jamie on to a certain extent, too. I had wanted to set-up and take to another level healthy eating and wholesome living as a way of life for Julian from the get-go, so that had been a new, enjoyable and rewarding experience for me, too.

BOOK FOUR:

SECONDS OUT, TIME-OUT

CHAPTER TWO

Towards the end of my maternity leave, I had the experience of having my two nieces, Tasha, eighteen, and Sara, thirteen, stay with me for a while. Tasha was six and a half months pregnant at the time, and Beverly, her mother, was in Africa for the second time with her new partner Lenny and their two-year-old daughter. The arrangement worked very well, perhaps because Tasha and Sara were essentially good girls and had already been a part of my life since they were babies. .

As part of the arrangement, Tasha would take up the paid role of sitter for Julian, an arrangement that made my return to work, thanks to the minimum of disruptions to Julian's routine, an exceptionally smooth one. The additional funds also gave Tasha the extra monies needed to buy the various things that she and her forthcoming child would need, and the extra icing on the cake was that Julian adjusted to the situation really well. I had feared that he wouldn't have, but I should have known that he would, as by nature he was a happy go lucky, easy to please and to get along with boy. Forever the comedian, he took great delight in making others laugh.

Before my return to work, I had assumed that Barbara would have changed, or at the very least have moved on in her ill will towards me. For me, it had come to be water under the bridge, so much so that when I returned to work, on the very first day, I took the opportunity to share my desire to get along better with her. However, to my utter surprise, and dismay, I found that Barbara was as adamant, as well as keen, to pick up where we left off. She wanted and intended, after a whole year, to continue as before. As such, as well as within the very same week of my arrival, in our first supervision meeting, right at the top of the agenda, was the three-month disciplinary action that she was pleased to let me know was still outstanding, by all of two weeks.

I was amazed, as I had truly believed that it was over and done with. She also went on to show me a report, which she had obviously worked very hard at compiling and completing, ready to hand to me. In it, she cited this and that about me, all fabrications and blatant same ol' lies dressed up as 'concerns.' She had also got Frank involved, whose mere input and involvement gave her credibility and a bony leg to stand on. Indeed, it was an input that had really thrown me; it had thrown me that Frank, a pastor of some sort in his outside of work life, could allow himself be used in that way, and to that extent.

Frank, who I had gone out my way to support and train,

especially when he first came into post, as well as subsequently, in spite of my initial and instinctual dislike of him. In spite of it, we had gone on to get along really well; there had been no contention between us, so I felt so utterly betrayed and bitterly disappointed with him for allowing himself to be misused in this way, and against me of all people!

I felt especially betrayed by Frank because, a month before I was due to return to work, I'd had this dream where I had embraced him and he had half-heartedly and reluctantly returned the embrace, which had left a distinct impression on me. That same afternoon, I had called him at work – I hadn't spoken to him since going on maternity leave – whereupon I relayed the dream to him, and asked if he and everything was OK. He had assured me that everything was fine between us.

The general idea of making me out to be incompetent at my job really infuriated me, as I loved my work and went to great pains to ensure that my clients got the most and best of me and the help that I was able to give. I guess Barbara knew exactly where and how to hurt me, which made me see how truly disturbed, bitter and twisted she was; to have spent a whole year mounting this case against me said as such. She really wanted me out, and perhaps she had hoped that I wouldn't have returned after giving birth and had this ready as her 'just in case,' being the very sad individual that she was. As for me, I would leave when I was good and ready, but I could have done without all of this.

Upon my return, I also found out that the situation between her and Mandy had escalated something terrible, and had resulted in Mandy being placed in another of the organisation's shop fronts. This was something that Mandy said Barbara was none too pleased with, as she had wanted her gone completely, which to a certain extent was understandable because, as Mandy herself had informed me, she had given Barbara a good ol' run for her money. In this instance, senior management had totally believed Mandy and taken her side.

At the time, there was someone else still in post that had come in to cover my maternity leave, and who was also filling in on Mandy's side of things until they found a replacement administrator. This was someone, it later came to be revealed, that Barbara had also had a hand in bringing to Intentions, who Barbara had ensured would therefore be sufficiently grateful enough to humour her; to do whatever she asked and wanted. She had asked this new worker to totally go over, recreate and replace with Barbara's new clinical instructions and materials, all the literature I had had a hand in creating.

A whole batch of new material was now in existence. I wouldn't mind if these replacement materials had, at the very least, made sense or were at all 'new and improved,' but they were all just Barbara's crazy, nonsensical ideas; ideas well out of keeping with the organisation's philosophy and way of working.

From where I (alone) was standing, Barbara had truly flipped her lid and lost the plot. She really believed that Intentions was her very own baby, and it did really hurt me to see how she just discarded and binned all my work, which I had put an awful lot of time, effort and energy into creating; ideas that had really worked well and had indeed helped Intentions get up on its feet, whereas Barbara's ideas were destined to bring the place, and all the good work, totally to its knees. Sadly, it was all about Barbara's needs and no one else's, and it was beginning to become crystal clear that if she couldn't have what she wanted, she was damned if she would let anyone else have it their way, whatever the cost.

What also totally pissed me off concerning this complete revamping of the work was the fact that they, and more specifically she, didn't even have the hindsight, intelligence or whatever it was that was needed to have taken out all traces of my ideas. Instead, they plagiarised large chunks of my ideas and then claimed them as her own at the bottom of the newly minted and signed acknowledgement page.

In some ways, I couldn't help but feel at times a certain pity for Barbara, as going by the way that she looked and behaved – she had large bags under her eyes and looked extremely worn out – you could tell that this was a woman, for whatever reason, utterly possessed. You could tell that she wasn't, and hadn't for a long time, been getting much, let alone good quality, sleep. And through Mandy, it came to my attention that she was still very much at odds with her own (new) line manager, as well as the overall senior management structure in general, and that she was getting on their last nerve, too.

So, for the first week of my return to work, it was very much a picking up from where we had left off, with her spending the weeks that followed – and me appealing – getting this new, yet old, crazy case written against me approved, and if possible, extended for an additional period. That was her work, and like I said, because of Frank's input giving her added credibility, as she knew it would, her line manager, who in hindsight seemed to have no other choice, agreed, that the disciplinary would remain in place, albeit just for the month that followed.

I felt so unsupported and somewhat defeated after having my appeal fall once again on deaf ears. At the time, I had thought that surely her line manager could see her real and true intentions; surely, he could see just where she was coming from, since they themselves had had their fair share of difficulties. I also knew that both he and senior management already knew her to be particularly nonsensical and unreasonable, so why they were still siding with her and allowing her to get away with murder, I had no idea.

With the disciplinary action fully approved and back in swing, Barbara continued her crazy-arse control dance, taking an even tighter rein and setting about taking total control and authority as much as she could. For example, directly after I had written up my client's session notes, she took it upon herself to check them out, which really pissed me off, however not for long, as I endeavoured to turn that particular situation around. I did so by going even further out of my way, as by the by I generally kept good, focussed, clear and concise case notes, to make those notes even more the work of art I thought they already were by my nature.

I went into great detail, taking care to give Barbara exactly what she needed from me, which in this instance was alcohol unit knowledge. I also went to great lengths to give her all that she needed to know and should herself have been taking better care of when working with her own clients, and indeed clients in general. I loved to write, so this exercise quickly became fun for me, and surprise, surprise, it wasn't too long before she stopped inspecting those case notes.

Also, as part of her Mission Impossible to take absolute control, she increased supervision sessions, a place where I also took the opportunity to behave similarly as I did with the client notes. So, she, as much as she wanted to, was unable to satisfactorily enjoy the kind of control and power that she wanted to have over me. Therefore, supervision went from bad to worse, becoming even more of a power-obsessed, contentious space. Even though I had shown her many times over that she *can't come test me* (a Jamaican terminology), Barbara still feverishly tried to pit her wits against mine.

Every morning, or more like afternoon, she would show up at work ready for war, looking even more tired and worn out than the day before.. She wouldn't give it up, though, and so I endeavoured to keep myself extremely positive, as well as spiritually protected. I had my readings, as well as the many positive affirmations and inspirational words that I kept around me, especially on my desk at work. One such affirmation that gave me great confidence and reassurance during this time said: **When you stand with the blessings of the Mother and God, it matters not who stands against you.**

I remember one time in supervision, as she was sitting there determined to tarnish and destroy my good name, just looking at her and clearly seeing the angry, hurtful and unhappy individual that she was, and within that moment of compassionate clear-seeing, I rather spontaneously said, trying to reach her, 'No matter what, and in spite of all this, Barbara, I still love you as a fellow human being – as a sister,' which made her even angrier. Later on, through the grapevine, I heard that she had told someone that during that particular supervision, I had made lewd advances towards her!

Anyway, and like already mentioned, after the year out, I felt truly refreshed and relaxed, as well as ever so happy and relieved with the babysitting arrangements that were working very well indeed. Julian didn't seem to be one bit fazed by my return to work, and on arriving back home the first thing I did was a breast feed, which became a good-quality bonding ritual each evening. I was also very happy to be getting into work on time at 9am, and sometimes even 8.40am, with relative ease. I'd had concerns about managing this, but not only was I managing very well, I would always be the first one in, even though I was the one who had just had a baby, as well as the only one with dependent children. I remember feeling quite chuffed about this.

Barbara's timekeeping, on the other hand, was getting worse by the day. On a good day, she wasn't able to get in until 10.15-10.30am, and on a bad day it would be 11. She hated this; she hated the fact that I could, would and did get in first, before she or any of her grateful steeds were in and willing to provide scrutiny. Frank didn't get in until 9.30am, although at times he managed ten-past or quarter-past nine, which meant that she couldn't 'get me' on my timekeeping. She had no choice but to take my word for it, as well as take my word that I was spending the mornings doing all the things she wanted me to do.

I could tell that it really hurt her being unable to have control of this particular situation, and like I said, that was mainly due to the fact that I had childcare down to a tee, as well as excellent time-management skills in general. I could also see that she was even upset with herself because she just couldn't get herself out of bed, as she was so very tired and way overspent. Indeed, if I had been her 'little girl inside,' I too would have been reluctant to get up and wake up into her life; to get up, wake up and greet Barbara's relentless, crazy, warmongering reality.

What she did do instead was call me up at 9am some mornings, and even though these calls were quite irritating at times, I came to find them quite amusing, and took to answering them in a bright and cheerful voice. One time, she got so frustrated with my early morning greeting cheer that she said words to the effect of, 'Don't speak to me like that!' which was an absolutely silly thing to say and to take and make issue with; a thing that we both knew in that moment sounded awfully ridiculous. She soon stopped making those early morning calls, too. Basically, that's how I endeavoured to deal with Barbara and the situation, with a sense of humour, as well as a generous pinch of salt. I also resolved not to let her bring me and my spirits down, especially not to her level.

One disturbing thing I did note immediately upon my return to work was the stark decline in the number of clients we saw on any given day; the list had drastically reduced. Before, when things were good, I would see at least four to six clients on an average day; once Frank had settled in, he would see around three to four, Sally, a volunteer alcohol counsellor I brought with me from Ijeomah, three to five and Barbara two to four, notwithstanding the unexpected referrals and drop-ins accessing our service from time to time.

Now, on most days, no one came, and when they did, it was in dribs and drabs; perhaps on average just two, three or four regular clients in a week. Indeed, Intentions had began to feel like a ghost town, and when I brought the diminished numbers fact to Frank's attention, he had, a little embarrassedly, tried to feign surprise; he had tried to make out that he hadn't noticed, and didn't know what I was talking about.

One other thing that Barbara did, which especially angered me, was to deliberately work against my resuming work with this one particular client, and indeed with all of my previous caseload. This particular client was one who I had been working with for as long as I had been at Intentions, right up to the time that I went on maternity leave. We had worked really well together, and she had made great progress, which was a really big deal considering the hell she had been through; it wasn't any wonder that she drank in an attempt to escape and numb the pain.

Anyway, the client had returned to Intentions knowing that I was due to return from maternity leave soon, whereupon Barbara maliciously turned down her request to continue sessions with me. She tried instead to get the client to work with Frank, which she did try for all of one session, before repeating her plea to continue work with me, but once again to no avail. Barbara's clearly deceptive reasoning for turning down the client's request, and in effect turning away a client, therefore failing to serve and meet her needs, was that it wasn't healthy or a good thing for clients to be dependent on one counsellor, which was absolute nonsense. It was all about control; all about Barbara trying to resume control of some situation she had come to believe she had lost control over.

It was pure and simple Barbarititis, and because Barbara had taken to keeping all the clients files under lock and key, especially mine, including all my old ones, there was no way I could contact the client and find a way to lessen the blow that I knew she had most unfairly received. She never came back again, and I was left completely understanding and knowing why Intentions was seeing hardly any clients at all. I was also mad now, as that shot was well below the belt.

During this work-related stressful time I met Everton and we went on to become really good friend. Everton used to work upstairs from us/Intentions in a separate organisation. He became a great source of support to me, being someone close by to talk to, particularly and immediately as certain things were unfolding.

Nearly every day we met for lunch, which he happily treated me to, and he also got into the habit of dropping me home at the end of the day. We also began a special ritual every Friday evening of chilling out with some African takeaway of pounded yam and fish, which we ate traditionally with our hands; something I really enjoyed and took to. The relationship was easy and effortless, and even when it became clear that he wanted more, he was patient and not pushy at all, at least to begin with.

In becoming my friend, Everton inadvertently became Barbara's enemy. In reaction to our budding friendship, she immediately tried to befriend him; to somehow get in between us and cast her spell, but it didn't work. Everton didn't entertain her in the slightest, as he was already very astonished, unhappy, disappointed and at times damn right angry with the way she was and had been behaving towards me; a thing on occasion he clearly saw for himself.

Everton had thus been a saving grace. I had been so longing for that kind of advocate and that particular kind of friendship, and when Barbara realised that her magic wasn't going to work on him, she then set about a mission to discredit him by instead befriending his boss and endeavouring to drive a wedge between Everton and him, but again to no avail.

Everton also liked to read, and it wasn't long before I had introduced him to the *Metu Neter*, which he, like me, took to feverishly. Basically, he, like me, became involved in the whole spiritual black consciousness movement. It was good to have someone likeminded to share my interests with, and it wasn't long before he began to accompany me to the Ausar Auset Society, a pan-African organisation developed to provide classes to help the African community better know and develop themselves spiritually, socially, psychologically, collectively and optimally. I had already been to a number of classes at the society, and had found them useful. I was already familiar with the ideas, as I had been studying the *Metu Neter* texts for some time by then, and before long Everton had also joined me in vegetarianism and later, also like me, becoming vegan and fasting at regular intervals.

Everton was an interesting character. He was of mixed parentage; father African and mother Scottish. He was born and raised in Scotland, so had a strong Scottish accent, as well as very long dreads; so long, in fact, that they fell way down his back, past his bottom. He was a very lively, friendly, caring, supportive and outgoing person; very different than any guy I had previously known. I loved his friendship.

Everton also used to send me nice cards with beautiful messages, in addition to buying me little gifts, looking at me with such desire and tell me how very beautiful he thought I was, and how happy he was to be knowing me. It used to feel too much, as well as embarrassing, at times; I so wasn't used to all that! However, it also used to feel, someplace deep inside, both reassuring and flattering whenever he behaved in that way. Still, in spite of all that, I didn't feel anything for him romantically. For me, at that particular time, the friendship was more than enough, so we carried on, and he carried on carrying the torch.

Back to Love

BOOK FOUR:

SECONDS OUT, TIME-OUT

CHAPTER THREE

Not too long after returning to work and being reintroduced
to the new heights of Barbara's madness, November 1997 to be
exact, I decided that it was time to move on, as I could see that
she was never going to let up, and I had truly grown tired and
bored of it; plus, she just wouldn't let me do any real work. By
then, Julian had been offered a nursery place and had settled in
very well, which had also meant that I had to leave work an hour
early to get down my side of town to pick him up; a thing Barbara
had also tried to sabotage. She tried to do this by objecting to me
skipping my lunch breaks in order to leave at 4pm.

However, Barbara's sabotage didn't work, as her line
manager rebuked her after seeing how destructive she was
being, encouraging her instead to be more sympathetic and
understanding by ensuring, at the very least, that I took a couple

of breaks since I'd be missing the lunch ones; reminding Barbara also that those twenty-minute mid-morning and afternoon breaks were something that all workers were entitled to.

With all this, and I guess in reaction to this current 'something else' feeling, I decided enough was enough, and began to keep my eyes opened for other vacancies. I also wanted something nearer to home, as well as part-time, although the thought of dropping hours did cause me some concern, mainly regarding whether I would be able to cope financially.

Before long, I came upon this job, which sounded to me so ideal, fitting nicely in with all the things I was then requiring. It was part-time and just down the road from me, as well as being a move up the vocational ladder. The position was for a counselling services manager at a , working for a small, but developing, specialised mental health service. I was so excited to have found it, and immediately applied.

I was ecstatic to find out that my application had been successful; that I had been shortlisted. Everything seemed to be going very well, and in the direction that I was choosing, as if the Creator had created this exit; this next page. The only problem, which almost brought me down from the high that I was on, was Barbara's promise of a bad reference, which she had dished out to others numerous times before. In our better days, she had actually told me, and shown me, a bad reference she had given, and she didn't even care at the time that it had gotten her into trouble.

Knowing Barbara, I knew that she wouldn't be able to not give me one; I knew that this would be her last weapon, and something that she'd have been looking forward to. The thing was, I had actually, and perhaps short-sightedly, made her a referee on the application form, but being someone who can think very speedily on her feet, upon finding out that the application had been successful, I immediately set about correcting that. I did so by contacting the place where I was applying for the position and telling them I had made a mistake, and then giving them Barbara's line manger as a reference instead.

I had asked him if it was OK for me to do this, as I had concerns about Barbara's ability to be objective and give me a sound reference, and he had been fine with it. He went on to give me such a glowing refcrence, acknowledging all the things I had developed during my time at Intentions – things that Barbara had tried to discredit and sabotage, particularly during the disciplinary meetings that he was also party to. I truly felt that justice had finally been served, and the record set straight, when he wrote that very positive and glowing reference for me. I felt that, finally, Intention's senior management had given me the support and understanding they should have offered a long time ago.

When Barbara realised that I had gone for a job and had been successful, needless to say, eagerly and gleefully she awaited the call for reference, to play her dirty hand. However, when she came to realise that it had been denied, and that I had gone over her head to her very own line manager, who had provided me with a very worthy reference in her place, she was none too pleased. Even though her managers had adamantly ignored her pleas of unfairness and all the rest, she still made one last-ditch attempt to sabotage me, which I found out about not too long after taking up the new post.

Incredibly, she had actually called up the organisation and given them her thoughts, feelings and reference anyway. Needless to say, at the time I was so incensed, and in response had called, informed and complained to her line manager, who assured me that he would take up the matter. He would also be informed a couple of weeks later, again by me, of another and similar defamation of character, after Barbara had set about deliberately spreading the word, through the black professionals 'small world' grapevine, which had promptly gotten back to me, that I had mental health problems, and as such shouldn't even be working in the caring profession with vulnerable clients!

It was obvious that the accusations had come directly from her, as the rumour had started through a close work colleague of hers, who she had once said similarly slanderous things about to me! This person had, in turn, gone on to share it as a matter of fact with various others linked to my new place of work, as well as with a close work college of mines, Janet Sanders from my BWACS days, with whom I still had professional links, and who had shared it all with me. All of this, I believe, created a certain doubt in my new line manager's mind, way before she had even got a chance to know me.

I was vexed, naturally, but not too vexed to see that never-the-Barbara-less, the victory had been mine; that I had had the last word in spite of those last-ditch sabotage attempts! It was good to have it draw to the conclusion that it did, and I couldn't have planned it better myself. Even though it was painful leaving Intentions on such a bad note; the bad note being that on the last day, and in the week leading up to it, not a single soul had acknowledged my leaving in the way I believe it should have been acknowledged. I had given Intentions a lot on all levels, and I had worked there for four years. I was just left to work out the door, like any other working day, without comment, let alone well wishes.

I was disappointed with Frank the most. I had hoped he would wake up and do the right thing in the end, what with him being a member of the clergy and all- he was a pastor of sorts and considering all the support I had given him and how we had previously got on well, in spite of my initial misgivings.

One day, in the midst of his ongoing betrayals and the heat of Barbara's madness, out of the blue I had taken him aside and had sincerely both enquired and stated to him, 'Frank, have me and you ever had anything?' He had thought about it, and rather ashamedly reported back an unequivocal, 'No,' to which I had further said, 'Have me and you ever crossed any bad words or anything of that sort?' and once again he admitted that we hadn't. At that point, I walked off and left him with his conscience.

That's how I had wanted to raise and leave the subject for his clergy conscience; he had to have one. I just wanted him to do his own maths; to know something that he was mature enough to know; to know the part we can and do play in (in effect) giving leverage, credibility and therefore power to absolute madness. Where was his personal responsibility to himself and wider responsibility towards me? Where was the good mind God had given him, a thing we are keen to take pride and affirm makes us, as humans, separate from and better than the animals? Please! Animals do animal perfectly; humans do humane atrociously.

The only good thing regarding the period of my actual departure was that I was able to leave a whole two weeks before the due date. Barbara's line manager had gone on to make that decision as things became so intolerable, unbearable and more out in the open between us, as she became a woman enraged by not getting her own way, and me, on the contrary, a woman terribly relieved, at peace and overjoyed to be on my way.

As such, and naturally, as Barbara became more obstinate and crazy, I became more vocal and instigative; very much less of the sufferer in silence biding my time. As she wound me up, I wound her right back, but she couldn't take it from me, whereas I had become immune to it from her. Her line manager got ever so fed up of her constant complaint calls and reports, as well as the ones I absolutely had to report myself.

He got so fed up with it all that he told me to leave; to remain until the end of the week – it had been a Tuesday – and then see out the rest of my notice at home; a thing that I was naturally ecstatic about, because it meant that I got a chance to recuperate and rest, with pay, before taking up my new post, which was icing on the cake!

Temporarily defeated, and trying desperately to gain some control even over that situation, Barbara tried to get me to go before the Friday. She had come to me the Wednesday, at the end of the day, and said that I didn't have to come back to work for the last two days. Naturally, I declined.

As a result of the positive turn of events, namely the securing of this new managerial part time post just up the road from me, 1998 started off really well. The only downside was that, although Everton had supported me throughout the whole of the ordeal, even buying me my first briefcase for my new job, a couple of months later, the relationship went to pot. Everton wanted more, but I just couldn't give it to him.

Maybe I could have in time, which I shared with him, as well as sharing with him the importance of me being able to have such a platonic friendship with him in the first place. To me, this was really important and healing in and of itself, and boy had I needed it, but for him it wasn't enough, and as time went by he became more pushy in his desire to have a more intimate and unified relationship with me. The more I tried to explain to him, first-hand as well as in an heartfelt letter, and reiterate that perhaps, given more time, something more intimate could develop, he just couldn't see or appreciate where I was coming from, which had been a real disappointment, because the relationship was very important to me.

In the end, when he still continued to persist and push, I had to say to him that if he wasn't happy or satisfied with the way things were, that perhaps he himself needed to consider the alternatives; that even though I didn't want him to end the relationship, I would have to respect his 'what would be best for him' decision. Whereupon, and rather angrily and disappointed, he chose to quit.

Although, to a certain extent, I understood his reaction and feelings, it angered me that he could just take off like that; that he could just disappear out of my life so swiftly and decidedly. Everton being able to do so made it seem to me that he just wanted what he wanted; that he hadn't valued the friendship and couldn't see what it meant to me. If he could see, then he had deliberately cut out of the relationship like that just to hurt me, like he perhaps thought I was deliberately hurting him, maybe...

By the by, I still remember Everton with a certain degree of fondness; he had been a very good source of support to me during the Barbara nightmare saga, and one that I would never forget, having received very little support from elsewhere. To give him credit, he did show up some five weeks later to see what could be rekindled, but it was already too late; we were most definitely at different emotional places by then, and the friendship had been left dented too long. So, not too long afterwards, we totally parted company.

Still, I had the new job to occupy and keep me company. Money did, as anticipated, become a bit of a struggle, but I struggled on, as I really enjoyed getting stuck in and doing my job as counselling service manager; it was my challenge. However, and sadly, before too long I began to have concerns, as I realised that the nature of the job was like early days BWACS: under-resourced, with one main person doing it all, and an over involved (female) Co-ordinator who was also Chair and Project the brain-child of; though a little different in the sense that we had quite a number of volunteers in place.

However, the volunteers all needed to be supervised, continually recruited and managed. Also, most of our volunteers were counsellors in training and very much babes in practise, let alone to the practise of assisting and supporting very vulnerable and deeply wounded service users.

BOOK FOUR:

SECONDS OUT, TIME-OUT

CHAPTER FOUR

After being in post for fourteen months, and having received a really good performance evaluation report, the coordinator and chair of the management committee felt I needed to spend more time outside the project, applying for and keeping abreast of whatever funding was available; the coordinator was a bit of a 'going after funding' junkie. Although I understood the need to secure further funding, I thought their ideas about me spending more time pursuing it somewhat unrealistic, what with me being the only paid worker, and part-time at that, responsible for carrying out and overseeing so many aspects of the service's delivery and development.

Instinctively, I knew that my being away from the office, off ground level, would do more harm than good, as well as undermine the smooth delivery of the much-needed structures that had been carefully put into place. To tell you the truth, I also hadn't had much experience of fundraising, so had felt more than a little out of my depth. Besides, it was the clients' needs that were paramount for me, and I truly believed that losing sight of this fact, in any shape or form, at that present developmental time would to do the service much more harm than good, all of which I endeavoured to relay to the chair, Mrs Bailey, but to no avail.

The committee had understood my concerns to a certain extent, but that's why we need further funding, they asserted. It was all very chicken and egg, which to a certain extent is to be expected with these types of under-resourced specialist service provisions. Still, their simultaneous hearing and not hearing what I was saying frustrated me, not least because there just wasn't enough time to focus on the things that needed to be focused on. When they finally got the message, they tried to remedy it by suggesting more hours; they were happy to find the money to increase my time to 25-30 hours a week. However, I was happy with the eighteen hours I was already doing and had no desire to change it.

I think I was getting tired; tired of having to do it all and of working within the same old dynamics, with the same old struggles and conflicts. I became even more tired when the coordinator tried to become that bit more domineering and autocratic, as I began to raise my concerns with what I felt were her unrealistic demands and lack of foresight in other key areas as well.

As I grew in confidence as a manager, I began to take and stand my ground, expressing more of my mind in certain situations, especially those I believed compromised the needs of our client group, all of which led to the power struggle taking a more definite shape. This was the same kind of struggle that I had already been forewarned had happened in the past between Mrs Bailey and all the previously employed (female) managers. When she began undermining and discrediting me in my absence, as well as presence, in committee meetings and in the presence of staff, I could feel another *enough is enough* coming. I could hear, 'Seconds out… time to depart.'

When I started work there I had resolved that the next time I was in a work situation, or otherwise, and those same old dynamics began to present themselves again and threaten to get out of hand, I would quit. The Barbara and Martha experiences had taught me this, so when an opportunity arose around that time, I grabbed it.

The opportunity came in regard to the restructuring of the whole early years child care provisions in Hackney, which meant a number of early years child care providers at that time came under certain threat in regard to funding, Julian's nursery included. This resulted in an increase in fees to try and make nursery ends meet, much to parents' and carers' dismay. I was on the nursery management committee at the time, acting as its chair, which was another demanding responsibility. So as the situation at work lingered on, I took that particular new nursery development to make my exit at work.

At the time, I had not too long started seeing my first private client for alcohol counselling, and had also been seriously thinking about developing my own ideas and initiatives, especially the idea of developing and delivering a women's dance therapy group, an idea inspired by my past involvement with the Ausar Auset Society, where I was first introduced to the Het-Heru healing dance. Dancing had always been a great passion of mine, so I was really excited about this.

The dance session would be something that I would provide through my continued liaisons with Janet Sanders, who had acted as chair when I was working at latter days BWACS, and had alerted me to Barbara's destructive rumours about my competence, or more precisely lack thereof, as a counsellor.

I was also working with Janet on doing some occasional sessional alcohol counselling work under BWACS' remit, as well as under her own service provision which she managed. Also, to keep BWACS active, as its funding had run out and as a provision it was just sitting upstairs doing nothing, I used its space for my entrepreneur endeavours. So, there was a pipeline, and much had already been set up in its regard.

At the time, I had thought that all of the experience and energy I had over the years put into developing other people's initiatives and ideas should now be put into developing and following my own; thinking how wonderful it would be to set about doing so without the conflict and hassle that had come with working for and with those various people. I knew I could fare and do better working for and on my own behalf, so in June 1999, I gave my notice, which had felt absolutely risky at the time, but nevertheless had been a risk I was willing to take.

The chair responsible for the total operation of the whole and larger organisation, as well as his coordinator and other committee members, were really sad to see me go. He felt that I had conducted myself well and had been truly professional, especially and considering the potential there had been for conflict. He said that even though he could see why I had to go – the reason for leaving I had given was that I could no longer afford nursery fees – the door would always be open if I ever wanted to come back.

Another member of the committee also said that she had known that they hadn't been wrong employing me, and was happy to have given me the benefit of the doubt. I had deciphered, from what she had said, that she had been referring to Barbara's initial sabotaging attempts. She, the secretary, had also said that generally, she had liked my style; the way I carried myself and went about my work. It had felt really good getting this kind of recognition and feedback from what seemed unlikely sources, what with them being 'elders' and all, and in my mind, much harder to please. Still, my mind was made up.

The volunteer counsellors, whose admiration and respect I had also managed to gain, expressed similar sentiments. Mrs Bailey, on the other hand, was a bit surprised when I gave in my notice, but I felt that before too long – by the end of that day, in fact – it had turned into a positive in her mind; perhaps for her own motives and reasons, or perhaps because that's how she deals with the unexpected; perhaps a bit of both.

Either way, and whatever the case, I always believed that Mrs Bailey had continued to distrust me after hearing Barbara out; that unlike the other larger committee members, she had not entirely given me the benefit of the doubt, even though I also felt that she couldn't help but respect me for all I had achieved in such a short period of time, and without great conflict with her or anyone else. I had worked there for seventeen months.

In particular regard to Mrs Bailey, and like I said, I had decided to leave before the potential for conflict had truly escalated to the scale it had with Martha and Barbara. I think she secretly admired my quiet, confident, professional and essentially peaceful manner, but all of that made little observable difference with her, mainly because all the positive things she felt towards me were unconscious and subject to negative, envious energy immediately following any good feelings about me. I could see this in her.

This I felt most keenly when she didn't seem to offer me a good and decent goodbye. The volunteers did, but she, as my superior, the one I was most accountable to, didn't see my leaving as significant in any way. Perhaps, in the final analysis, how people behave has more to do with them and their way of dealing with things more than with anything else. However, and either way, in my heart of hearts, I wished that she had been different in this regard. I wished that she, like Barbara, had truly acknowledged me and my parting. I wished that they could have risen up out of 'their stuff' long enough to do the bigger thing.

My suspicions were confirmed in regard to Mrs Bailey's general and underlying suspicious, distrustful and negative energy towards me, when on my very last day, while I was collecting my personal belongings, she took to hovering; hovering and almost stalking me, as if I would take things that I oughtn't. Even the admin and a couple of other volunteers noticed the humiliating and embarrassing way in which she was behaving. Her behaviour made me feel like a thief, even though I wasn't stealing, which made me feel both angry and unreasonably ashamed. By the same token, however, I also felt overjoyed to be out of there; that freedom couldn't have come a second sooner!

Before my final departure, during the final week of working out my notice, I met Norman Norvil. He had come to the project as one of Mrs Bailey's contacts to provide training to the volunteer counsellors, arranged out of our training budget. Not that we needed this particular type of training he offered, but the admin had told me that Norman had come in before when I wasn't around, and that he was 'fine,' so when I heard he was visiting again, I made sure that I would be around to take a peek.

When the day came, I introduced myself to Norman and arranged a time to meet with him and provide a one-to-one update and handover in regard to what I thought, as soon to be ex-manager, the volunteer counsellors could most benefit from with his particular training package, among other things.

Norman was very fine indeed. He was tall, with smooth, caramel-coloured skin and was both charming and good-looking. He had such grace and style, but he was also, I later found out, fifteen years my senior, though he certainly didn't look it. He was so very pleasing to the eye, and I was so attracted to him that at the end of the meeting I gave him my contact details and he gave me his, each promising most definitely to be in touch, and both very much looking forward to our next meeting.

As promised, Norman and I did meet up and explored ways in which we could work together, but before too long I let my feelings known to him, whereupon he had said that he was not too long out of a relationship, so wasn't really looking for a commitment as such, at this current time at least. That was a bit disappointing to have found out, but I guess a little part of me rationalised, *Maybe he'll change his mind, especially after getting to know me.*

Despite him saying that, we dated, I think. We met up and went on quite a number of dates, from dancing and eating out to attending various business conventions, all of which had been great fun. I had enjoyed going out dancing with Norman the most, for as strait-laced as he at first appeared, he knew how to let go and move his body. We soon became an item.

Over time Norman allowed himself to become influenced by some of my spiritual practices, even going on to put together a spiritual alter of sorts in his own home. For a time, it seemed as if the budding of some kind of faith was being restored within him, but before too long cracks begun to show. I began to notice that as I became more relaxed within the relationship and within myself, whenever I expressed a different opinion than his, he became quite hostile. At first it was quite subtle, but I would differently be left feeling like I had been stung, though not quite able to put my finger on it: it was all very underhand and confusing.

Before then, I had, more unconsciously, picked up on the need, while in his company, to please him by being agreeable and keeping certain opinions to myself. I had unconsciously detected that voicing differences in opinion was not allowed and would rock an already not-too-steady or secure boat. I had felt someplace that being more out spoken would cause conflict..

As I began to more fully express my thoughts, my feelings and the way I understood and saw things, conflicts grew. During those times, and rather craftily, he would try and manipulate me back around to his way of thinking. I could see what he was doing; I had suspected it and had had my fair share of experiences, all my life it seemed, of characters just like him, but he really became quite mentally undermining, treating me, and acting as if I was 'the client' and he was 'the know it all' therapist. However, I stood my ground.

After the first time that type of dirty fighting conflict happened, we kind of did and didn't reach a resolution, and I was left with a distinctively bitter taste in my mouth. When a similar incident then occurred, within the next four days to be exact, and be became that bit more manipulative, controlling, patronising and verbally aggressive than before, I reassured myself that if it continued, I would be gone, which it did, and I was.

Like I said, and the good Lord knows, by that time I'd had my fair share of angry, manipulative, dominating, controlling spirits, and as such had become too well-versed in the likes of it to be taken in, let alone along for a ride, though he had tried. If the karmatic reasons for their being in my life were to help me (further) develop a back bone- and find my voice, by then I had; thanks! Also, because Norman was much older than me, and oh so 'educated,' which he was very proud of and had been keen to share, I had expected more. I had expected better from him. I didn't expect to run into this hurtful, vengeful, angry, manipulative little boy (spirit).

Because of the differences in age, I did at times notice during the relationship, a part of me kept getting him mixed up with my father, which had also brought with it an accompanying fear and feeling that I shouldn't oppose him; that I had to take care to keep the peace and please him, just in case he turned. These feelings and fears had unnerved me; had made me feel terribly scared in a cut off, faraway place; feelings that had made me feel like I wasn't his equal, even as I stood up to him; feelings and fears that had made me feel more like an insecure little girl.

During our eight-month relationship Norman also used to want to do things during sex that I was not at all into, and a couple of times, under duress, I gave in, both times ending up feeling absolutely disgusted, as well as totally taken advantage of; hating it, and in that moment hating him, too. As much as I did hate it, and despite knowing that those feelings in and of themselves were totally valid, I also noted that it felt disproportionate to the situation at hand; that it felt reminiscent of past childhood violations; that something had be triggered.

During the last 'put upon time,' I remember getting up in the middle of the night as he slept, feeling totally sick to the stomach. My tummy truly ached, as someplace, outside of full awareness, I moved around the house, feeling dazed, disorientated and alone... I was again a feral child who hadn't quite figured out what it was she needed, exactly, but was hoping to find something that would make her, me, feel more, happy and whole, instead of filled with such inner, empty desperateness. Someone to help her, me to feel… more real…more   human...

Mixed in with all this was the distant feeling and memory of a great big act of betrayal; of the coming upon a significant other who misread her, my signals, taking total advantage and stealing that which was not his to take, in that moment making innocence and the need for love and comfort something hurtful, ugly, bitter, twisted, dirty; making neediness shameful and secret, and bringing with it a painful cloud of confusion, weighted with the wretchedness of those mixed feelings of getting *something*, though not *the thing* most needed…

That night I was "triggered," or as psychodynamic therapy would term it, was in a state of regression, albeit, unconsciously.

On the surface, in the topside world, all I keenly felt was sick, troubled and disgusted, psychosomatically going on afterwards to experience and suffer with acute vaginal discomfort and a bad and recurrent case of cystitis. The good detective within me had made a mental note of all this, instinctively feeling and knowing that doing so would prove, again, useful one day, and also instinctively knowing and working under the premise that life has to have all the missing pieces in order to bring me healing and make me whole again- as whole as I can possibly be.

When the relationship with Norman ended, I was left with such angry and hurtful feelings, especially when I looked back and saw how much I had compromised myself, and how manipulative he was and had sought to be. I felt tricked and cheated, for he was not at all as he presented, which made the total experience of him and us disillusioning and extremely disappointing. The experience of Norman was like being starving and hungry and biting into a big shiny red apple, but then upon biting in deep, realising that the apple was rotten. I was left feeling disgusted, having taken him in.

Consequently, being the writer that I am, it had given me great pleasure and relief putting it all in a letter to him, especially letting him know that in future, when someone says no to any one of his sexual preferences, he should listen to them rather than twist their arm, like he had done with me. In the letter, I let him know the full range of my feelings, and it was only at that point that I felt the relationship had truly ended.

The end of disappointing relationships always brought with it lots of difficult feelings: painful bitter bile tasting feelings. In regard to Norman, these feelings were particularly intense, which I was finding really difficult to cope with, let alone put away and in the same old ways. Perhaps this was even more difficult because I no longer had the option of eating or smoking the pain away.

At the time, April 2000, I had also been keeping a dream journal for just over a year, and when I found the time to truly look over and study it, I was surprised to have found that at least 80 percent of it spoke to the theme of childhood sexual abuse. Thus far, I had only been aware of and consciously dealt with the now ex family friend's abuse of me. The others hadn't seemed as impacting, even though they were, because they happened mostly with so-called strangers and consisted mostly of groping.

However, the dream journal mentioned other incidents with other vaguely familiar known and unknown people, like this couple I used to stay with when my mum was away. I must have been about seven, eight or nine at the time, and I stayed with them quite often. Barry, the husband, had a similar look and cultural heritage as Norman. I had always had vague, fragmented memories of being in the bed with Barry when the wife was out, and him trying to do something to me...

I suspect that 'something' was the same thing I had experienced with Norman, which I had tried not to focus on or put two and two together, but the dream, in its own way, said as much using the stored memory. What I had remembered the most from that incident, from that memory, was the red carpet in the room and my feeling hungry, needy and wanting, so perhaps being desirous of the advances and in effect causing it; immaturely rationalising that in as such, I do not have the right to feel that to be an injury, let alone be angry about it. Squaring it in my head like that as children often do...

I am not sure if the abuse took place the once, twice or many more times. Or it happened that one time I was staying at their house and was awakened out of my sleep by the noise of their loving making. That incident sticks in my mind because when she had had enough and wanted the intercourse to end, and he didn't, he had hit her, and she had gotten dressed and stormed out of the house late at night, staying away until late the next morning.

The memory of that particular situation had been initially, however fleetingly, triggered in 1991while actively dealing with the ex-family friend abuse of me during therapy. However, even at this particular time, while reading the dream journal, I was still quite distant from it all, mostly because of the unconscious and misguided self-blame, still outside of awareness, taking place. It wasn't until August 2005, while working on this book, that it became plain as the light of day what Barry had done, and in its wake brought to the surface other, previously out of reach memories and feelings.

It was those particular feelings and memories, and daring to share them and it all with a friend, especially post the Norman experience, which had led me to the decision of further therapy. My friend had suggested that I seek out some kind of therapy to help put these particular demons to bed, which I agreed with and did, and which took me, in June 2000, right back into group therapy at the Women's Therapy Centre, the very place where I had started this recovery journey. At the time, it had felt like a coming to full circle, like moving further into the deeper healing and inner knowing, and in so doing, bringing more needed completion to the beginning of ends.

BOOK FOUR:

SECONDS OUT, TIME-OUT

CHAPTER FIVE

Although it had been experiences with Norman that had brought me to the group, my most conscious reason for being there was to get a better understanding of relationships and the part I did and didn't play within them, to either my detriment or benefit. Also, because I wasn't using marijuana as crutch this time around in my therapeutic endeavours, I was hoping that the journey would take me that bit further; that bit deeper into the healing process.

Not that I had forgotten that it had been the sexual abuse and their memories that had prompted my reaching out for therapy again, but at that time, at the beginning and middle of the group psychotherapy, I wasn't quite ready to face it head-on. It was like I had fallen asleep on the childhood sexual abuse issue again, but then perhaps that was all part of the process, and I had to deal with some other things first before I could go there.

One of the important lessons I learned in the group at the time was how, most of the time, psychological defences- habitual ways of thinking, feeling and behaving when stressed or experiencing internal and external conflict, are developed first and foremost out of the human need of self- protection. These 'defences' are self-preserving in development and nature, acting as survival mechanisms that as human beings we have at our disposal as we make our way through this experience called life. Thank God for them.

I also learned that, essentially, these defences – my own, my mother's and other people's that I had the mis/fortune to run into – are, rather than being designed to hurt, there to preserve and protect my oftentimes precarious senses of self. The more severe, traumatic, unsafe and reoccurring early childhood adverse experiences are, the more intense and almost insurmountable these defences can be to overcome later on. Contrary to popular belief, I came to see that I could not simply 'move on' and 'put, once and for all, traumatic experiences behind me.

Therefore, it brought great relief for me to so clearly see that a lot of the pain others had caused me, it wasn't, and isn't, intentional. Sadly, most of the time these mechanisms are hidden from view having been 'decided' upon years ago in the most formative and vulnerable years, and then continuing over a significant period of time, becoming deeply ingrained and very much a part of the personality and its makeup. This I came to truly understand and to better see, before reaching the conclusion that it wasn't *me* that my mother, Norman, Mark or even my so-called uncle Nigel hated, despite their hateful behaviour toward me.

Instead, I realised, that hurtful, destructive energy came from *within* them. Through this understanding, or 'overstanding,' as Rastafarians on occasion have termed it, I was also able to see that I didn't deserve to be hated and hurt, which was a thing that I had come to believe because their behaviour, at that time, made no sense to me, other than maybe this, which was a thing I could try and correct, if it was indeed my fault...

As a child, and more unconsciously as an adult, I couldn't see any other reason why these people were treating me as they did, other than that I was undeserving and unworthy, especially as however good and accommodating I tried so very hard to be, the assaults and insults just kept coming.

The dawning idea that it wasn't personal, and that I wasn't in the first place irredeemably bad and to blame, released something deep within the very core of me. The budding realization that these ill-feelings belonged to them and were results of their own bitter and twisted defences, which they had endeavoured to put onto me and to come at me with, was truly liberating to say the least, as well as deeply healing.

A similar defence mechanism of projection, displacement and scapegoating is acted out under the label of sexism, racism, and other isms; the inferiority complex lies with the perpetrator carrying this irrational- unconscious- hate and unhealed psychological pain, that feels so unbearable it needs an *anyway* out. Not that I am excusing bad behaviour, far from it.

I truly, consciously and most definitely, began to comprehend all these things in the group setting, as well as through the group experience and its dynamics, and through the stories we shared, and through being aware and observing how other people and their particular coping mechanisms and defences had come to be in the first place. Within the group itself, I came to see how our own individual defence mechanisms interacted between us, both positively and negatively, as well as generally and at times compulsively in spite of OUR best efforts to resolve them. I also had the privilege of observing how particular inner demons acted themselves out.

A lot of the work in the group involved grief therapy, which is reactivating and bringing to a certain consciousness and conclusion, and therefore resolution, the grieving process; the 'all that was loss' being consciously and compassionately acknowledged; 'the thing' that my compulsion to repeat certain, often painful, experiences had endeavoured to resolve in its own unique and out of date way. There were a lot of things that needed coming to terms with personally, as well as collectively in the group.

For all of us there, myself very much included, it was the grieving of a childhood lost that needed the most coming to terms with. Indeed, on a number of occasions, I had seriously wondered how much of a reality 'childhood' and its ideals actually were for the majority of people in this world.

Still, grieve for a childhood lost I did, seeing as though the part of the world I live in claims it to be my right; claims childhood to be a well and true part of life, and as such has put in place all kinds of laws to supposedly ensure, oversee and protect that basic human right. As such, I grew up expecting to have had a proper childhood, which I hadn't. Instead, I had spent my whole childhood mostly waiting for 'childhood' to begin, as well as despairing when it didn't.

I had also spent my whole childhood fearing, knowing and feeling that my childhood innocence had already been spoiled, along with the hope of ever truly relaxing, feeling safe and free and enjoying childhood, because of the level and degree of sexual abuse, abandonment and neglect I had suffered and endured. The socio-economical, cultural and psychological odds had been stacked quite a bit against me. That was an existential truth and social reality for the likes of me.

Not that there hadn't been any place where childhood hadn't come into play, as after all, I was indeed a child. These occasions just felt and seemed few and far between, as well as terribly overcast by certain inevitabilities that had made it seem far safer, and became easier, for me to forsake the hurtful company of others and remain mostly on my own, in my own self-created world. Adults became such bad news for me; not just those called family, but also, growing up in the 1970s, those racists, I feared, were lurking around street corners in the social atmosphere, ready to pounce on me because of the colour of my skin, which was another thing I had no way of controlling.

In the group, I also began to grieve the fact that I had spent what felt like the better part of childhood and early adult life trying to undo and redo the past; trying to cover over its wounds and scars the only way I knew how. I had to grieve the loss of what I could have been doing and being instead; grieving the loss of the life and dreams I could have been living if things had somehow been different. Without self-loving confidence, as the Jamaican activist Marcus Garvey said, black people are twice defeated in the race of life.

Grieving was a very big task for me; one difficult to embrace, especially when there's so much rage, as well as a desire for revenge, notwithstanding the desire to cover it over with 'forgive and forgets,' rather than growing through the pain. At that time in the group, having to bear, feel and relive those very intense archaic associated feelings wasn't, and isn't, easy. However, as someone knowing the recovery process once wisely said, *'The only way out is through.'* For the sake of inner growth, and for mental and emotional well-being, one has to try and put those demons to bed.

The grief work of legitimising, as well as accepting and letting the pain in and go, and getting the whole process and balance right; not staying with it for longer than is wise or putting it too soon behind, was and is a most awesome and harrowing of tasks. This is particularly so when the thing being grieved is more emotional/psychological in kind (unseen to the naked eye) and belonging to another time, all of which makes it real difficult to share with others, especially when people and the world are quick to respond and say, 'It's the past; get over it now; put it away;' the most hurtful words to hear, even if saying so is well-intentioned, when moving past it is what is exactly trying to be satisfactorily accomplished by talking about it.

The recovery process is a very harrowing process along road less travelled precisely for that fact. So anyone taking this this road is no less than hero and Brave-Heart in my book- as I was discovering I am in the therapy group at this time.

During the group sessions, I also struggled generally with fully facing and accepting the full magnitude of all that had happened to me, let alone emotionally connecting to the whole damned feeling experience of it. It is an experience that sometimes feels like the process of giving birth in that you are happy because you want the baby and the joy of the all that you imagine being a mother and rising a child in love will bring and be, but just at that moment, in the moment of truth and of the dream becoming reality, the pain becomes incredibly unbearable, making you angry and tempted to think you were crazy for ever wanting this in the first place, knowing you have already come too far to turn back now.

This is where I was, on another level and very much at the forefront of grief, yet at the same time far from full delivery of the hoped-for dream of holding 'deep and lasting' peace and inner well-being. I was still reading a lot, a lot of self-help books, as well as all of the major names in the metaphysical and spiritual fields.

Reworking my inner and outer world, not just in the group but all the time, had been the forward thrusting, uncompromising movement in my life back then. A tenacious spirit deep within me wanting to give and get and learn the best from any situation I found myself in, refusing to let past negative experiences continue to get the better of me. That's how it felt to be in the battle I was in; the arduous and very worthwhile weaving together of an altogether more harmonious and cohesive inside-out life.

I also began to work on myself at a bodily level during the time of the group, especially when I began to realise how difficult it was for me to relax, to feel and to just be at home and at peace in my own skin. This uneasiness, I began to notice, occurred around simple tasks such as taking a bath.

Indeed, generally I came to discover how fearful I felt towards my body, especially being in and with its nakedness, as if it had something wrong with it and in it, a thing that I later went on to conclude wasn't at all surprising, considering how others had taken advantage of it. I guess, inadvertently, I had also come to somehow feel betrayed and let down by it, especially when it had naturally responded and took what it needed from unwholesome life experiences.

Even ordinary sensations frightened me, making a certain part of me fear them and wonder if it, and thus I, was sick; if I sooner, rather than later, would get sick and die before I'd truly had the chance to fully live. So much in the area of body, feelings, instincts and sensations had been injured, but thankfully not beyond repair. Having had not a single reliable adult to help me with these things, there was much I didn't understand, and therefore was still just as confused about as I had been as a child.

During this time, it also became easy to see how smoking weed, and indeed problem eating, acted to numb and distract me from what was truly and really unresolved and hurting inside. It's like before this time I had been more like a 'head;' a head hiding from the hole in its heart. Now, I had to lose my mind; to get sufficiently out of my head and come back to my good senses, which at the time was a very scary place to be: myself and my body. It seemed a scary place after a lifetime of swallowing back down this and that; of redirecting anger, dissatisfaction, fear and pain to a more manageable 'intellectual' plane, as well as under that humongous proverbial mountain carpet. I was re/learning and relearning loads.

BOOK FIVE:

MAKING LIGHT

CHAPTER ONE

"We shall not cease from exploration, and the end of all our exploring will be to arrive where we started and know the place for the first time," **T. S. Elliot.**

In September 2001, I decided to take my writing to another level, that is, other than just writing in my journals. I did so by joining a 'Life into Fiction' writing course at Centreprise, in Dalston, Hackney. The course turned out to be very beneficial as well as truly interesting, though in the beginning it took the usual period of time for me not to feel terribly nervous and uneasy all the time. Once I settled, though, the whole group ended up working really well together. The tutor was excellent and kept the whole course focused, relevant and fun.

The course appealed to me mainly because I wanted to find a way to use my journals to tell my life story, and also because ever since I was a little girl, I had been writing and toying with the idea of writing books, so this was and had been very much a childhood dream. The course then was just another one of my projects; another one of my creative pursuits resulting from my big toe being in the pool of life-exploring. Being on a time-out therefore came to be like being in this wonderful creative playground, with all my most favourite playthings.

During the course, even though the initial thought was to write my life story using my journals, I ended up writing poetry, an infatuation and preoccupation that continued well into 2004, which also saw me on stage performing at a number of venues – an incredible experience, and I might add, achievement, in and of itself. As the weeks went by on the course, I was truly encouraged to receive some really good feedback on the work I created, which boosted my self-esteem no end.

Also, at the time I had become a bit infatuated with this guy who was also on the course, so much so that one day I plucked up the courage to tell him so. The idea of having a relationship with someone who seemed to be inclined towards creativity, and to the task of expressing his innermost self and ideas in this way, excited me beyond all measure, and made me think that perhaps this could be the man of my dreams.

His name was Stanley, and he used to drop me home after classes. I so used to look forward to those lifts once they became a regular occurrence, as I enjoyed sharing moments in time with him. He also had good taste in music, another thing about him that excited me, as it was important that the man for me, like me, also appreciated good music. So, during this time I also got him to make me some music tapes, as even though I loved music, my collection had, in the preceding years, along with the music-loving and dancing side of myself, taken a bit of a nosedive.

It was Valentine's Day when I plucked up the courage to let him know how I was feeling about him, which for me took some doing. His response was a little disappointing, though; he thanked me for the card, and that was all. This had left me a little confused, as he had seemed interested and had been quite flirty with me, but still wasn't actively putting himself out there. However, I continued to take the initiative, since he wasn't giving me the total brush off, either.

We went out a couple of times, the first being for a drink on the back of my Valentine's Day declaration, and also in response to his wanting to share something with me. However, it came to pass that even then he wasn't terribly forthcoming and clear about the something he had wanted to share, so I had to decipher it myself. What I believe that he was trying to tell me was that he had not too long come out of a long-term relationship, one that had nearly ended in marriage, and as such, at the present time, he wasn't looking for anything too serious.

I had told him previously that I had been single two years and was looking for something more meaningful, and I think he was trying to tell me that that wasn't what he was wanting with me, although he was probably still toying with the idea of something or another, hence my confusion. Also, he used to say things like he would not be good for my health, and joke that his love was 'poison;' the same poison Pink sang about on a tape he had done for me and similarly titled.

In a sense, I'm glad nothing happened between us, because he seemed to have been most definitely a ladies man, and even though a part of me didn't at first notice it, or didn't want to notice, I was still in the habit of falling under the spell of the fairy tale way of believing that, through my love, I could change a man; that I could make princes out of frogs. However, while the class lasted, Stanley continued to be a secret fantasy and obsession of mine, a thing which at times became very painful, as it was a situation that could not be made reality no matter how much yearned for it; for the love of a good man. Needless to say, I was still so very lonely in the department of male-female, adult-adult reciprocal love relationship.

Around the same time, on February 27th 2002, at 3.02am, my grandson, Matthias Isaiah Jones-Raymond, Mattie for short, was born, weighing in at 6lbs 12oz. I had become a grandmother at the tender age of 37, and a very happy one at that.

It had been quite a shock initially, finding out that I would be a granny, but it was a reality that I soon adjusted to. The night that Jamie and his girlfriend broke the news to me, I was fast asleep when the phone rang, and he came onto the line saying, 'Mum, I have some good news and some bad news. The bad news is that Chantelle's pregnant, and the good news is that you are going to be a grandmother.' It was as simple and straightforward as that. Jamie was eighteen years old at the time, and nineteen when he became a dad. His girlfriend Chantelle was just eleven months older.

I didn't say much about it at first, as it was around midnight and I was still half-asleep; indeed, a part of me came off the phone wondering if it had all been a dream. However, when I came to in the morning and was more able to separate fact from fantasy, it all began to dawn on me. It wasn't a dream; I was to become granny, and my child a father. When I had awoken, Jamie and Chantelle were already there, together, waiting to have a face-to-face conversation about it.

Jamie and Chantelle had looked really nervous, perhaps anticipating conflict of some sort, and I was a bit naughty, drawing it out by taking my good ol' time to get washed and ready first. I suppose I did that – took my time – because there was no conflict to have. What was done had already been done; it was already out of my hands, as the unfolding of our children's lives, and all human life, oftentimes is. Then, when I was ready, I approached them and broached the subject, putting them out of their apparent unease.

Initially, it was a shock, but being an adaptive person that soon passed, though it was immediately replaced by fretting and worrying; fret and worry as the 'mother of the son' who had got some other woman's daughter pregnant. I became very concerned with how Chantelle's mother would receive the news, and the fretting kept hold, even though Chantelle and Jamie had already been dating for a couple of years at the time. My fears also increased somewhat when they told me that Chantelle's mother wanted to meet with me.

My fear was that she was coming to curse me out for somehow allowing my son to impregnate her daughter, but to my surprise, the meeting was far from aggressive or hostile. We met at my house; whereupon I went on to find out that she was actually happy to have a boy like Jamie be the father of her daughter's child. I was so happy and relieved at how smooth and easy it all went.

As soon-to-be-grandparents, we were both very happy, willing and committed to play our respective parts, supporting them as best we could as the young parents they were to become. Jamie and Chantelle had also showed great levels of maturity and responsibility during the pregnancy, and Jamie had religiously accompanied Chantelle to all of her antenatal appointments, already taking to his new role with a mature sense of responsibility.

They had also been preparing for the baby by buying all the items they would need, which amounted to quite a number of things. They both seemed to be stepping up so well, and I remembering observing this and feeling a slight twinge of jealously at how well they were doing and had achieved together already; he had put my baby fathers to shame. Most of all, though, I felt very proud of Jamie, as it seemed he had learned something about being a father in spite of not having had a wholly responsible one himself.

I had also felt, not too long after they told me they were expecting a baby, that perhaps, like me, Jamie could use the experience of being a father to pull his socks up and become a bit clearer about what he wanted from life, and the part he saw himself playing in order to get it, especially in regard to a career. In that area of his life, I felt that he had not quite yet found his feet or moved in any committed and direct way towards a particular end, at times to my dismay.

I say to my dismay, because I could see how capable he was, and I could also see the lack of confidence that got in the way of him allowing himself to truly go for it by actively seeking out employment in a more sustained way. Even at school, Jamie hadn't stretched himself too much, especially when he felt that he didn't have to. It was like he knew how capable he was and that was enough for him, but that self-assurance wasn't enough to allow him to leave secondary school with the grades he was more than capable of achieving.

Sadly, and most regrettably, and I believe particularly so to him as well as to me, even though he'd persisted with the football for quite a while, Jamie stopped going when he turned fifteen. He stopped mainly, I believe, because I had my hands full with work and with becoming a single parent again, and as such didn't really having the time or energy to support him and football in the way that I had been able to before; that particular support and push that children oftentimes need to continue pursuing, rather than giving up on, those important, potentially life-changing, dreams and ambitions.

I also believe that if he'd had support coming from the direction of his dad, who never saw him play, and he was such a great player, Jamie would have continued. Even in this regard, I wished I had thought to do more; to have also encouraged and seen to it that his father was there to support him in his football years. With the right support, I believe Jamie could have gone quite far, and at the very least, like some of his friends from football, made it to a professional league.

After leaving school and being out of that environment for a while, Jamie had started going to these raves with his father, a thing I was far from happy about because, to me, it meant trying to lead a high-profile lifestyle; it meant making sure that one had the money to have the latest name-brand clothes; to have the latest lick and look, as well as the bottles of champagne that was generally required at these raves. The crowd was also much older than Jamie, which had concerned me.

To my mind, at the time, I had seen those raves, and his father, as far from desirable influences. I used to take these concerns into the therapy group, but I knew that there was not much I could do. In effect, it was all about a little boy still needing, wanting and now following his dad. Sometimes, we take the food we need wherever we can find it.

It had been my hope that after Jamie had finished and had done relatively well in school that he would go on to college, and then into higher education. Like I said, he was more than capable, and as such had the potential. As a child, I had made such conscious efforts to engage him and get him to be of independent, and out-of-the-box, thought and action; to be of great self-knowing and intelligence, which at that time, like a sponge, he had soaked up well. However, what you want for your children sometimes does not coincide, at particular times, with the things they want for themselves...

This time-out period of creativity and the following of dreams felt also to be a time of allowing and giving myself a second childhood of sorts. This period of time created a space for self-exploration and play – a space I hadn't quite had before, what with my childhood being what it was. Plus, coming from the kind of environment that I did, as a child I didn't feel that I could relax enough to freely play, so during this time, I continued to give myself this much needed space to be, play and create, as well as to perform my poetry.

On the writing course, I had met Peter Price and when the course finished, we continued to remain in contact, building up a friendship. He'd taken a similar path to my own, initially seeking out the course for creative story writing and then going down the poetry route instead. He also went on to organise and run his own poetry nights for new comers like ourselves, and I performed at a number of his events over the two to three years that followed. I also performed at many other venues.

Essentially, my poems grew out of the desire to truly grasp the particular 'insight' coming out of any given situation or experience that I would be going and growing through at the time; that was my inspiration. Therefore, my poems were, at heart, quite personal in nature, and in having that quality, my hope was that they would be relevant to any human being at this particular time in history, especially those similar to me, struggling with their own inner demons and harrowing processes of realising lasting change.

While performing, I used the name 'Insperience,' which was not only my stage name, but had also been the name I had delivered my counselling and workshop practises under. It was my desire to continue the work of 'making a difference,' even within my creative and artistic endeavours, so I wanted there to be a direct link between my creative writings and the therapeutic work that had been, and still was, what I consider to be my life's work.

It was an awesome experience to create my poetry, mainly because I had such a wealth of experience/insperience to draw on, and my creative juices were truly overflowing, running from still waters in inner wells so deep. It was like discovering a never-ending source of something that I myself could take in and drink from, and use to create the opportunity to feed other souls with. I love to give and to spread love, peace and joy; it truly fills me up.

Wholesome giving fills me up and out, making me, and everything I had been through, worthwhile and worthy. It makes life seem and feel more like a joy, putting me back in touch with the innocent, beautiful childlike self that forever is and always will be me. I had such creative aptitude, altitude and appetite that creating my work inadvertently made that once menacing inner-emptiness feel ever so full and satisfied; full of good true life, most of the time, all of which was an exciting and new self-development.

Not that creative work is easy. Indeed, at the best of times, creating my poems had been a frustrating endeavour, especially trying to find and bring into certain light the right image, sentence or word; doing so not only to make sense of for one's self, but also to make digestible material that is appetising for the crowd; for whatever particular audience is at hand at any given time. That was hard, although ultimately worthwhile.

The creative process is truly a challenge in and of itself, which at times came to be experienced by myself as a kind of obsession; an all-encompassing and time-consuming experience. However, like I said, it was more than worth it- though I do not recall holding this enlightened perspective that much in the more trying moments of creativity. Therefore, being patient with the process, in time, also became a focus and very much a work in progress. My creative expressions, along with everything else on this journey, provided me with the necessary character-building, life-affirming and sustaining experience; for me, much-needed, life vital, ***all that have soul***-food vitamins.

The emergence of this creative self, which I guess had already emerged to a certain extent from the initial decision I made to be on this ***back to self-love*** path, was here re-emerging and therefore better establishing itself; making its presence more known and felt through my creative works, a thing that I could feel was putting me in touch with a deeper, more vulnerable and authentic side of myself, which was great, as this side of myself had been previously lost to me.

Performing my poems, on the other hand, was a much bigger challenge, for it always came with a crippling sense of self-consciousness; one that had so plagued me since childhood, having me believing how terribly inadequate and lacking I was. It was because of this that, even though as a child and growing adolescent I had so loved music and dancing, whenever I performed it was always within this crippling state of great self-consciousness, which resulted in me giving up particular dreams that involved being on stage, or in any way in front of an audience.

In my younger days, when I used to perform, and especially if it was dancing, I would get so terribly nervous and anxious. My legs would shake, at times uncontrollably, which made me even more self-conscious, embarrassed and ashamed; ashamed mostly because I thought people could see how scared, defective and embarrassed I was, because I just couldn't control it or make the nervous shaking stop. Also, being by nature quite a sensitive child, having had hyper-insensitive and critical parents obviously didn't help any.

Naturally, as a sensitive child, I took these past, now automatic, pervasive toxic thought patterns around with me on the life stage, as well as into the world of performance poetry, projecting them onto any audience. However, I didn't let it stop me from sharing my work and pleasing myself in this way, as stretching myself was more pressing and important than the fear of doing so. For me at that time, it was most definitely as Henry Thoreau once wisely advised, *'Don't die with your music in you!'*

There was no way, as hard as the journey got at times, that I would die with my music unreleased, in whatever little and unique way it happened to manifest. Thus, I decided that, at the very least, I would die trying to make sure that certain dreams came to some sort of fruition, and it was this desire, this determination and this drive that I took into my creative writing and the field of performance poetry, regardless of how anxiety-stricken and fear-riddled I felt during virtually each and every performance.

I knew that I was doing the right thing, and that I was indeed on a very good track, when at the end of each performance I was left wanting more. Like the Teletubbies, a part of me would exclaim, 'Again! Again! Again!' which had been evidence enough for me that in spite of everything, I must continue on. Each time I performed, the nerves lessened, and although they always lingered to some extent, in retrospect that is perfectly well and good.

After a good while, I decided to take time out from performance poetry, with the last time I performed a piece being spring 2004. Not that I had sat down at that time and consciously arrived at that decision; I just felt that I needed some kind of pause. I felt like I needed to learn and see something more, knowing someplace that I would be a stronger person and better performer for it. Also, to be totally honest, as much as I enjoyed the overall experience, I wasn't altogether happy with some of the venues I performed in.

I didn't always feel that being so open, honest and giving in those places was 'the place' for it, and had begun to seriously wonder if those environments had also added to my general and overall insecurity and nerves. I had begun to notice that certain places, like your wine bars and such, seemed to prefer more 'light entertainment,' which is fair enough. I began to also feel that perhaps there was someplace else for me to be with my poems; that perhaps places out there existed and waited for me, with audiences more open and willing to hear and receive the good news of what it means to be a fully feeling and breathing human being, and how totally awesome and beautiful that is: to simply **Be**, as intended.

Perhaps those particular audiences were people in the business, process and work of healing and recovery; those who had more consciously happened along this road themselves. I wasn't quite sure; all I knew was a pause was at hand. After all, I had happened on this particular poetry path by accident, if there's really ever such a thing, since the reason I had joined the writing course in the first place to was to write my life story.

Back to Love

BOOK FIVE:

MAKING LIGHT

CHAPTER TWO

With the good feelings I was getting from creating, singing, dancing and performing my poems, I began to feel that I was indeed living the life of my dreams; that I, and things, had truly taken off and were flying high. There were a number of courses that I was looking forward to taking up in the coming September of 2003, such as a writing course to get back into the idea of story writing and working towards getting my life's story in print, and a musicianship course to help with my singing through reading and understanding music..

After successfully completing the preceding year's Singing with Confidence class, I was to start on the next level up. The only problem was that the writing course I wanted to start fell on a Wednesday, which clashed with the therapy group. The group met Wednesday mornings, 10.00-11.30am, but because I felt things had truly changed and were taking off, I decided, in the two months preceding the start of these courses, to work towards ending the group therapy.

Within the group, I had also felt that overall things in my life were quiet and settled, which at that time made the idea of leaving seem genuinely OK, and like it was the right thing do. Additionally, the idea of leaving had been coming up on and off for me anyway, especially after the Easter break, so after being in the group for three years, I gave in my notice officially at the beginning of July 2003. Ideally, a month's notice was asked for as a good period of time to say goodbye and deal with some of the issues that endings can bring, so I did just that.

Overall, it had been a heartfelt ending; it had felt like the home-leaving I never had. It felt like I was flying the nest, which brought up how disappointing and wanting my actual leaving home had been. There had been not one single adult – no mother or anybody else – to witness and be party to it, so the group's acknowledged and heartfelt goodbye was a kind of blessing in itself, and helped bring that specific experience of abandonment to the fore, which I was, in the group, able to explore and mourn, before putting the experience to rest.

When my new courses started, I was in full swing. Well, for about three to four weeks that is, as before too long, the end of October, it all began to feel way too much. It began to feel like I had bitten off much more than I could chew, as in reality, I was doing far too many courses; three on one day, two of which I had to come back to do in the evening, leaving the City Lit at 9.30pm. Also, the singing course, continuing in the more operatic classical style, was not the kind of singing I really wanted to be doing. I had actually been more interested in doing the jazz, blues and soul singing class, but had felt like I wouldn't have been qualified enough to get on that course, so I had bottled out.

Plus, the idea and reality of leaving my house in the evening was not something that I enjoyed at the best of times. I liked and preferred being at home with Julian, especially on a school night, and not being what felt like 'all the way up there' in Covent Garden, so one day, I decided to just quit the singing and musicianship classes, shortly followed by the writing course, which didn't seem to be my cup of tea, either. These were decisions that I both was and wasn't happy with, partly because it had also meant cutting losses. I had paid for all courses right up to the end of term, and here I was cutting out three weeks in.

Overall, even though quitting was a thing that I was not well-versed in doing, the decision to do so felt more right than wrong; it felt wholesome. On the whole, it felt and seemed as though I had gotten carried away with myself; that I had run way too far ahead. At the time, I had still been performing, cruising and enjoying the poetry circuit, secretly hoping that I would find the ideal mate along the way, especially now that I was enjoying more of a social life thanks to Shirley, my reliable and ever ready and available sitter, who lived just at the top of the road from me. I was still very much single and celibate following the Norman experience.

Anyway, two weeks down the road from quitting the courses, I decided instead to do a Helping in Schools course, in the hope of becoming somewhere in the not too distant future a classroom assistant. I had kind of decided that, when I returned to the world of so-called work, I wanted to work more with children, as well as within the school setting, so that I could get the holidays off and still be available to and for Julian. Home and family life, as well as space and time for creative expression and endeavours, had to come first, and everything else had to fit neatly in and around it.

I had considered at first becoming a trained teacher, but had wanted to have more one-to-one contact and interaction with children, still hoping and wanting to make more of an impact and difference where it was most psychosocially needed when working with people. I had thought that being a teacher would lessen this possibility, plus the time, energy and resources needed for teacher training would have put a strain on me that I just hadn't wanted or needed, so I decided against it. Helping in Schools was, while intensive, only a ten-week course, and it came to be an interesting and enjoyably experience, in which the tutor was exceptional and we, the course participants, worked well as a group.

Once the course began to draw towards an end, I began to miss the therapy group, and soon began to feel the need even more for it, like I hadn't quite finished with it, or it with me, even though at the time I had thought it to be the case. I still felt very much emotionally unsupported and alone, and I could see clearly how trust remained a great big issue for me; how the relationships issue I had wanted to use the group experience to overcome still lingered on strong.

I also felt that there were deeper things still in need of being resolved, even though I wasn't quite sure and couldn't exactly put my finger on what those particular things could be; the particular things that had brought me to the group, and had taken a certain nosedive while I had been exploring my creative side.

Those feelings of need and the unresolved got so bad during this time that I started to seriously think that maybe my leaving the group had been a bit premature. So, in the December of that year, 2003, just three months post-leaving the group, I contacted the Women's Therapy Centre via a letter to Anna, the group therapist, and in it shared my feelings straight from the heart; the full and true range of my feelings and my 'in hindsight' realisations, whereupon Anna invited me to see her to discuss it all in the new year, which I did.

When I spoke with Anna, my intention was to see if, through her, I could get some kind of individual therapy, but she suggested that perhaps I could think more about returning to the group instead. She, like me, felt that there was still more to be gained there, and that I could still benefit from letting my guard down at bit more and being supported that little bit further. She felt that, although I had used the group well enough, more often than not I had brought to it the more capable, self-sufficient, contained and competent Marcia. She felt that there was more to be had for the side of me that felt quite the opposite, all of which was absolutely true.

I had been working through my journals in the hope of using them to write a book, and I was also recording my dreams in the hope of learning something; something that still seemed amiss; something that still seemed to elude me, all of which had grown out of the Norman experience. During that time, in the group there had been a period where I had allowed that vulnerability to show, and allowed the group to see and support that side of me.

Indeed, I remember crying for a period of time, almost every week, which had continued on and off for at least a couple of months or so. However, while I was going through all that, I was never quite sure why I was crying. Anna had also said as much at the time, and as such she wasn't able to really understand my tears herself.

Oftentimes in therapy, I have expected the therapist to know what I'm struggling with, how I'm feeling and what I mean without me having to say it, like the therapist is an omnipotent, all-knowing and understanding mother. Like I said previously, this is the transference in operation, a thing that doesn't only limit itself to the therapeutic encounter, but occurs in all relationships, especially when we are feeling like a helpless little baby, vulnerable and in need of that particular kind of mothering, understanding and holding. I believe that the tears then were more unconscious in nature, coming from experiences long forgotten and buried, and yet needing to be more consciously grasped and grappled with; more directly owned and acknowledged.

Even though the idea of returning to the group freaked me out a little, making me think and feel like I would be viewed a fool for leaving in the first place, and a failure for returning, especially so soon, I still decided to go ahead with it. The awful thing was that it turned out to be a much longer wait than Anna had first anticipated and assumed. She had thought that I'd be able to return by the end of January, but she changed that date to the middle of February and then again until after the Easter break. In the end, it didn't happen until the May 2004, due to the group going through a difficult patch and needing space and time to work itself out, as well as get used to the idea of my return.

I also suspected that one particular group member, with whom I'd had my fair share of group dynamic power struggles, would have been experiencing conflict regarding my coming back, which I later found out she had. It was all part of the group process and work, which Anna wanted to get just right for the benefit of everyone, but knowing this did not detract from how psychologically agonising a wait it had been for me.

When I was finally able to return, I got stuck right in, as time became of the essence and the desire to get once and for all to the bottom of things took on new meaning. I was determined to put in 100 percent and express the full range of my experience and self. I was decided and determined that this was it; that I would learn to trust enough and let others in, even if it killed me, which in a sense it did. It came to kill more of the who I was not, and in so doing, make more room for the who I was still very much becoming.

Within just two months of my re-joining the group, while someone else was sharing their story during a session, I began to recall fragments of a dream I'd had around the time I'd started to weep my heart out, back when I hadn't realised what those tears were for.

My father was in the dream, and he had just rejected me for another; he was in bed with someone else, which left me feeling so wounded, and which had then, in the next scene, turned into Julian drowning in the sea. I couldn't save him, which seemed to break my heart completely. Instead, in Julian's place, I had been left with this weighty little girl sitting dripping wet on my lap, a girl, who I intuited in the dream, still needed my care and love.

There, in the dream, had started the weeping – a deep, heartfelt and heart-broken weeping, which had woken me out of my sleep, and that, in the next group meeting, that very same morning, I went onto relay to the others.

Upon hearing the dream, Anna had partially interpreted it as meaning that perhaps the lively, open, innocent and unspoiled part that Julian represented in the dream, which had drowned, was perhaps my own untapped potential; the kind of person and spirit that I initially was, before the wonder turned into a great, gaping and hurting hole. Perhaps, she suggested, the little girl left in its place in the dream represented the weight of those wounds, through which I thusly became the want for nothing, independent, capable and self-sufficient Marcia, or words to that effect.

These interpretations and speculations heralded the re-emergence of partially forgotten material; of a skeleton that had once been so totally closeted and hidden, but which had now begun to make its unconscious presence more consciously felt within a month or two of my return to the group, triggered that day by another group member sharing her own suspicions of childhood sexual molestation.

Group discussions had arrived at the theme of father-daughter incest after this particular member had relayed a dream she'd had regarding that issue during the week. In regard to herself, she couldn't recall any one particular incident while she was growing up, but ever since she could remember, her dreams had indicated as much. At the time, she just couldn't understand the dream, and was asking Anna what it could all mean.

I'd had similar dreams myself, past and present, as well as suspicions concerning my own father, but I had thought it all too egregious to believe, let alone actively explore. However, after Marjorie had shared her concerns, I followed suit, and even after so doing, I still at that stage somehow remained in what seemed like an age-old 'disbelief' that anything of that sort could or ever did happen.

These were similar feelings of disbelief that I had previously felt in past therapies, particularly when I had shared memories that spoke directly to the extent of the neglect, abandonment and deprivation that I had experienced as a child, as well as other previous childhood sexual abuse experiences. Somehow, those experiences had also come to be, and to feel, normal, rather than seen as the crimes and betrayals that they were. After all, doesn't everybody go through this? What's the big deal? We were still very lucky, because some people have it much worse -laminations my mother oftentimes spouted, internalised.

Therapeutic discussions and disclosures along the lines of the above oftentimes brought with them depersonalised feelings of being unreal or of little value, like the things they revealed couldn't have happened or didn't really; that I was just bellyaching and making much ado about nothing. It was like that part of me was nothing and had been trained to feel nothing.

Indeed, anything that was considered 'serious' pertaining to me was difficult for me to receive as such. It was just so difficult holding onto the fact that I mattered enough to be upset, affected and incensed by the things that had happened to me and had once caused me deep misery, before I'd found a way to do away with the pain for my own survival.

At the time, I also began to get in touch with some other very deep and painful feelings and memories; memories and feelings that provided the backdrop to the very conditions that the abuse had taken place within. I began to become totally in touch with and aware of how it had all *felt* and had been for me in childhood. I had found myself, at this particular time in therapy, at the very heart of an inner, utter desperation; at the heart of the desolate meandering of my childhood years, not feeling that I belonged to anyone, any time or any place.

I began to remember things like ritualistically sitting in the local laundry, bored and looking for something to do on those very long, lonely days; sitting in the laundry just to be around people, hoping they would 'see' me and take pity on me, and perhaps give me something, like money for food, sweets or my dollies. I must have been nine or ten years old at the time.

I also remembered spending an equal amount of time just staring out of the window at home; staring out on many an occasion at this family who lived a couple of gardens away and seemed to have it all: Mummy, Daddy, white, middle-class, money… unlike me and my broken family. Unlike me, who had so desperately wished to have had a piece of their pie, instead having to make do with daydream highs. However, even the experience of staring out of the bedroom window with my daydreams got spoiled, when one summer the father of the family became aware of my gaze and started making innuendos before going on to fondle himself….

I remember being five, six, seven, eight and nine years old, being and playing on my own. Sometimes, I did have friends, and best friends, too. Even at the best of times, though, I had keenly felt a certain distance and difference from them, what with my family being the way it was, and the feelings of alienation, separation from the human race.

At that time, I also used to be engaged in a lot of pretend play, mainly pretending that I had long hair and that I belonged to another family altogether – a more loving, caring and happy family, like the one in *Little House on the Prairie*. Also, at the time, the only thing that seemed real to me was my dolls. I loved my dolls and so loved getting totally absorbed in playing with them.

Overall it always felt much safer in my own little world; the one I retreated into and had created for myself, rather than the so-called 'real' world, where people and things couldn't be trusted and where happiness never seemed to last long, and therefore it and them shouldn't and couldn't be depended on.

It was a monstrous task to try and put into words these key early and late childhood experiences and feelings. It had been a very hard thing to try and do and stay with, although stay with it I had to, as the floodgates had been flung open. The experience of endeavouring to relay it all had at times felt as big, wide and vast as the sky itself, as well as everything outside and beyond it. In my sharing, I oftentimes felt that I was not doing my existence at that time full justice; words didn't seem to adequately fit it.

It was like at that time, in the group and in my childhood past, I was in another place, a different world and realm, which spoke an altogether different language and had an altogether different way of seeing, being and understanding. I guess you could say that I felt very much a stranger in the group, both within myself and within the experience. It was the same stranger I had identified as in my childhood, like no one really knew me as I was now getting to know myself.

The group work and healing experience at this time took me completely into another place and time. It all very much felt like time had slowed down, and that I was living in some kind of twilight zone; a space and place that housed great wells of sadness and pain, and saw me crying earnestly in many group sessions to come.

I was crying and becoming more and more out of touch with the coping, competent, self-sufficient and contained Marcia, and more and more in touch with all that was most vulnerable and real, and hurting within me. It was like I actually became that thrown away little girl again, and that I was, for the first time, most definitely feeling her pain, especially how it had been and had truly felt for her – for me – during that childhood time.

Having the group there for me as a real presence of support, which understood and cared about me and my well-being, made the process of transformation and change at that most critical and precarious moment in time a truly healing and awakening experience. Also, as my suspicions of my father's sexual abuse of me took more root, my sister Karen, on my dad's side, began to come more firmly into mind.

BOOK FIVE:

MAKING LIGHT

CHAPTER THREE

When I had stayed at my father's house in my teens, Karen had been there, too, living with him. According to my father, he had rescued her from a bad situation in Jamaica; he said that her mother had abandoned her, so he went and got her and brought her to England. Anyway, even though he painted himself as the knight in shining armour, I distinctly remember him treating her very badly, as well as like his personal slave.

One time, he beat her in front of me. I was in such shock to see him lose control like that, especially when he set about kicking her like some kind of dog, drawing blood. She was about fifteen or sixteen at the time, and I would have been about thirteen. Also, the very last time I vomited as a result of my bulimia, well after I had stopped doing it regularly, had been in response to a situation involving him.

It was during the first year of my degree course. I had had him, my mum and her friend around at mine for dinner, and during the course of the evening, I had showed him some work that I had been doing on the course. I guess I was feeling proud of myself, and as such was looking for his approval on a piece that I had been doing for a Women's Studies class.

Anyway, as he looked through it, he suddenly switched on me, just like he used to switch up on me when I stayed with him… the same exact way Mark, Julian's dad did He would fly into a rage for what seemed like no reason at all. Even with me now, in this situation, being an adult – I was twenty-three at the time- his behaviour made absolutely no sense. I just couldn't understand where he was coming from and why he was behaving in the way he was.

He began severely criticising and rubbishing my work. My mum wasn't in the room, or was more in and out, and he was carrying on in front of her friend, saying things like, 'Young people don't even know what they are talking about. What do they know about life and struggles, and how is Women's Studies going to help?'

Continuing on with his verbally and emotionally abusive behaviour, he said that I couldn't even spell because I had misspelled 'father,' and how stupid did that make me. I had felt totally flabbergasted and so terribly belittled; feelings I had felt before with him as a child, when he had behaved similarly whenever the mood took him.

I had also shared my work with him because he was always going on while I was growing up about how important education is. He was always, albeit in the most insensitive of ways, encouraging us – Karen, me and his other children – to expand our horizons and pursue the higher education side of the equation. Here I was doing just that, even after having a child at a young age, and he was carrying on like this!

At the time, I could tell that my mum's friend was also very taken aback by his behaviour; very uncomfortable and embarrassed. I could also tell that she felt sorry for me, and in my defence, she tried to cushion and rebuke what he was saying, offering some positive praise. It disturbed her so much that during the week she called my mum and told her how he was carrying on, and my mother brought it back to me, though we did not get into it.

I remember, at the time, that it had felt good to know that Cheryl, my mother's friend, had found his behaviour disturbing, too. I say this because, while we were growing up, I never really liked Cheryl. She used to be very mean to her daughter, calling her names in front of all and sundry, so much so that my heart used to go out to the girl, while my distrust, dislike, fear and silent rage burned for Cheryl. On a few occasions, Cheryl would turn her insensitivity on me, so I learned quick to stay away from her as a child.

Anyway, it was after my father, Cheryl and my mother had left that I had felt totally compelled to binge and gorge myself, before promptly vomiting it all back up. Being the good psychological detective that I can sometimes instinctively be, during the binge-purge act, I had known that what had taken place, and how I was now reacting to it all, were significantly linked.

What got in the way of these past experiences and memories and further confused things, and also made me want to contact Karen, was the fact that over the preceding four years, and especially post-graduation, my father and I had become quite close and appeared to be growing closer. Indeed, we kept regular enough contact, and we were close in the sense that he was there and was someone parental and key who I could talk to and get some understanding from. He was on standby as the parent I could talk to and get some childhood information from, and this felt both crucial and good because it had been hard getting anything out of my mother. In addition to this, I guess somewhere inside, a little girl still needed and craved her father's acceptance, love and approval.

I also felt sorry for him, for he had managed to isolate and estrange himself from all five of his children. All of his children's mothers seemed to have had some kind of deep-rooted emotional problem, all having abandoned their children in one way or the other. Anyway, through their rejection of him, he was becoming a very unhappy and lonely middle-aged man. Not that he saw himself like that, as in his own mind he was Mr Perfect, never at fault.

The reason he had given for his children's estrangement was due to their troubled past and maternal neglect and abandonment, I guess myself included, although he held me quietly up as the 'good one.' Since I remained neutral, being Little Miss Peaceful, he thought I was on his side, and so he made me the exception, which to that little lost child inside of me was enough. Perhaps that in itself was love...

The most of his children disliked him with a passion, and I had heard through the grapevine that Karen had a particular story and an additional reason for hating him. Having heard and known this, I had at various and at certain times over the years thought to get her number and make contact, but then I'd never felt the need to put that thought into definite action. I had also felt sorry for my father because of his own history, the one he had shared, which I had, from my own observations, gone on to connect to other bits and pieces of information about him, reading between the lines.

My father had experienced physical abuse at the hands of his father. Due to the domestic violence, his mother eventually left her husband and went to live with her sisters; his five aunts. All this happened in Jamaica before she came over to England on the Windrush. Also, whilst living with their aunts, whenever my father misbehaved, he had been disciplined in the most humiliating ways by his aunties, who I was told detested men and all had the upper hand in their marriages. I was told that one of the ways my father would be disciplined was by being made to wear female clothes and walk around the streets of Jamaica…

Similar to my mother and her traumatic childhood, what I did feel overall towards my father was a kind of painful pity, as I could see what he had been through and could tell that he found relationships particularly difficult, and as such was ending up a desperate loner. So, I swallowed a lot of the other stuff and settled for being the one that would bring to him acceptance, understanding and love; things that I believed he needed and craved.

Indeed, I felt more like the parent in regard to both my parents, and like I said, tied up in that back-to-front dynamic were the hopes of a parent-starved little girl; the hopes that one day, perhaps having learned from her, they would give her back some of the very same spoken and considered things that she gave to them willingly and freely.

However, even though we appeared close and it gave me a certain satisfaction, the relationship, was completely lopsided, with me doing all the listening and him all the talking, which was all very draining, as well as overwhelming at times, because he could half go on. I've even fallen asleep whilst listening to his ranting and ravings about people, and one time, when he had suspected that I had indeed just fallen asleep, he had carried on speaking regardless, rather than getting off the phone and letting me get some much needed shut eye!

When I was a child, he used to go on and on, this time about me and how he really felt about my mother, and the kind of mother he thought she was. His ranting, raving and swearing then, and especially as I got older, made me angry and made me feel vengeful, like I could just shoot his fucking brains out; like I wanted to stomp all over his face and kick him all over the place.

He could have such a vile and dirty mouth; such a wicked and evil tongue, and that could even be putting it lightly! I think, in the beginning of the father-child relationship, his rages just used to scare the shit out of me, but like I said, later on they just left me wanting to give him back as good as he gave.

Anyway, during our 'then' relationship, I had hoped we were getting close, and that perhaps I had put in enough of something to have finally gained a place in his heart. I used to share my poems with him as a way to get in and get some kind of acknowledgement and praise, and overall, he received them well, and had seemed glad that I was healing, growing, writing and performing.

On another level, though, this had confused me, because if he had done what he'd done, and somewhere I had known it, why would he be happy for me to be on this healing journey? Why didn't it threaten him? Did he think that I would never have remembered and addressed what he had done to me at some point? Did we make some kind of (unconscious) agreement to keep it in the past, and just between ourselves? What was going on?

There was ambivalence at his end when I went into therapy in 1991. The place I went for therapy at that time was just up the road from him, and it was also during the time that Nigel had taken, on occasion, to following me to therapy, and when his sexual abuse of me had come to full light. Anyway, at that time, my dad said to me once in conversation that I should be careful with therapy, and that it could turn you crazy. He had definitely tried to put me off it back then. I had noted that.

Another thing that came to mind during that particular time of incest disclosure, which had made me definitely make up my mind about making contact with Karen, was the time I shared with my father the ex-family friend sexual abuse of me…

At the time, we were having one of those chats about the past. He had initiated the conversation by speaking about the past himself; about the time of his and my mother's meeting, and especially about how he had become aware that I was his child. According to him, he had been in prison and had just been released, whereupon not too long afterwards, Monty, my mother's then boyfriend, had told him that I could be, and very possibly was, his daughter.

Monty had done so, according to my dad, after remarking to my mother that I looked more like Terence, my father, than the other suspect. I am not quite sure exactly how old I was at the time that Monty allegedly brought this information to my father's attention since, like already mentioned, my mother is not open to discussing things of the past, especially things like these, which perhaps shouldn't come as a surprise.

Anyway, I figure that I would have been about three years old at the time. My dad couldn't exactly remember my age himself, but from what he'd said, which I picked up on, he wasn't altogether convinced that I was his child but still went along with it, I think more because he figured that if he did go along with it, there could be a chance for he and my mother to become an item. My mother had also said as much, but never too much, in a conversation she initiated and was happy to have one time.

What she had also said was that after getting to know my supposed father for a short while the first time, she had had no intention of having anything lasting with him, as he was an out-and-out ladies' man. In regard to paternity, my father said to me that because the other guy in question was tall, skinny and light-skinned, he thought that he was more likely the father; that's how he became my dad.

The first time I was introduced to my father, it had been extremely hard to accept him as 'Dad,' as I had found him generally unappealing. I actually thought he was ugly, and he definitely wasn't as good-looking as some of the other guys that my mother surrounded herself with and was in the habit of dating. Not that my initial reaction was just about 'looks' per se; he just seemed ugly in a weird and 'off' kind of way. I just didn't like him; my spirit didn't take to him. Plus, the fact of him being introduced to me as Dad, just like that, took some getting used to.

At that time, I had taken to thinking that the father of my two sisters, Terri and Lauren, was my dad. I really would have preferred that their dad was mine, too, as in my eyes, he was ever so handsome: light-skinned, tall, good-looking, friendly and always delicious smelling. He always wore lovely smelling aftershave, which acted as (his) 'trade mark.'

It took great effort to accept him as my father, and even later as an adult, I still didn't quite know what and how to think of him or be with him, or even what to call him. I saw that it was the same for him, too: uncomfortable. Even as an adult, and as close as I thought we had gotten, he would often say, rather hesitantly, whenever I picked up the phone to take his call, 'Hello Marcia, it's Terrence… your father.' Actually, towards the end he was getting a bit more relaxed about just announcing himself to me as 'Dad.'

When I was a child, because he wanted to impress my mother and get in her good books, he did manage to earn the title of 'best father of the bunch,' and he did this by taking me out and having me stay over for periods at a time at his house, especially when my mother was abroad. He also used to give regular money to my mother and buy me clothes, jewellery and such. However, like I said, and as my mother had also said, when he had finally plucked up the courage to ask my mother for another chance, she turned him down, which I suspect would have wounded his male pride...

This was something that I definitely picked up on and concluded during the conversation that he had felt wounded, especially when he went on to immediately share with me how manipulative, controlling and conniving he had generally been in his pursuits and relationships with women, my mother included. He did this in the process of glorifying himself in my presence, without realising exactly what he was saying, or indeed what it said about him.

My father oftentimes shared and said certain inappropriate things with me as both adult and child. In this particular conversation, he shared details of the lengths to which he would go to 'get' his women. He shared how he used to prey upon and secure his women by deliberately choosing the vulnerable and most wounded, becoming their trusted confidant and getting inside their heads and straight to the heart of their discontent. Then, he would set about wooing them, giving them what he had deduced they most would need, all with a view to making them his. He completely 'psyched' them out, which I guess is how he earned the nickname 'Doc,' short for Doctor. That's what everyone called him. He also dabbled in the field of psychology and had some good basic knowledge to use to advantage!

His aim was always high, considering he wasn't terribly attractive, but then he sure was slick, dressed finely to the hilt, very sharp and intelligent, and also 'with it.' He would go after the beautiful, the educated, the strong-headed, the aspiring, but also, like I said, all women very vulnerable and insecure inside.

He would almost deliberately reach for the unattainable for the sheer challenge of it, and delight in the pseudo power it afforded him when his launch was successful. It was of these types that all of his children's mothers had been made.

He told me all of this ever so openly and proudly, and as with certain other information I heard, but was not quite ready at the time to do anything with, I tucked it away somewhere deep inside for safe keeping. It was like he had forgotten, during the conversation, that I was also his daughter, and a woman, and like I said, he couldn't quite see or step out of himself long enough to comprehend how unfavourable and downright despicable those revelations made him appear.

As we spoke, he also went on to share the reason why he took me out a lot and tried to do different things with me. He said he did so because in the very beginning, when he used to visit me as a child, it was like my mum didn't know what to do with us kids. To him, it was like she just basically had us there, and after attending to our most basic of needs, she didn't seem to have much else to do with us, and so left us to own devices, to entertain ourselves.

He said that I had been and seemed quite cut off from the rest, as well as inhibited and shy in my own little space, world and time. Hearing that had made me feel validated, because that was how I felt childhood had been for me; that's how lonely and desperate my existence had felt and seemed. I hadn't imagined it, because here he was confirming it. He told the story like he had indeed come to the rescue of poor, little ol' me, a story, like I said, he tells about each and every last one of his children; a story that in actual fact does contain that tiny grain of truth, though he then went on to further traumatise us all.

Like I said, it was during this conversation that I rather spontaneously disclosed the sexual abuse and it was his reaction, which at the time I had put down to him being concerned for me, that I would eventually remember in a new light, and which made me know that I had to make contact with my sister Karen. As I was telling him what the ex-family friend had done, he became visibly, as well as increasingly, fidgety and uncomfortable, so much so that by the time I had disclosed everything, all he could do to remain seated on his chair was sit at the very edge of it.

Like I said, at that time I had thought that perhaps he was behaving in this way because it was difficult for him to sit still and hear and accept the terrible thing done to his little girl, even though after the disclosure he didn't do or say anything in particular to confirm those thoughts. What he had done was to go straight on to talk about the time he had gone to Jamaica to 'rescue' Karen, whom he had seriously suspected had been sexually molested herself. There was no anger towards the abuser, who he knew very well and was in similar circle of friends; no sign of an, 'Oh my God, I am so sorry you went through that!'

The whole uncomfortable, fidgety initial reaction of his made me now, as I was putting the pieces together, wonder if he indeed had feared at that time that I was about to oust him and take him to task, which also made me additionally wonder if somewhere, outside of conscious awareness, I knew exactly what I was doing then, too. I wondered if, like any good detective, I was and had been slowly, perseveringly and patiently biding my time, all the while gathering evidence. And as some wise soul once said, ***God Can Heal A Broken Heart, but you need to give God all the pieces.***

I contacted Karen.

BOOK FIVE:

MAKING LIGHT

CHAPTER FOUR

Karen and I met the day after I made the call. It was Thursday morning, September 9th 2004, and after taking Julian to school, I had taken the tube straight to Oakwood, where she lived. She had also just dropped her children off for the day, one at school and the other at nursery, and we met at the train station before deciding that we would go talk and have a little something to eat at a café nearby.

I didn't eat much, as I'd already had breakfast, so we shared a little light conversation as I bided my time while she ate. Once she had finished, it seemed that the time had come for us to talk. I hadn't said that much to her on the phone ahead of the meeting, just that I needed to talk to her about our father. So, I took a deep breath and got straight to the subject. I could see she was concerned.

I told her what had triggered my call to her; the feeling that my father had sexually abused me, and I also shared a bit about the whole circumstances that had brought me to that conclusion, as well as my generally being on the road towards a certain recovery. We had only met twice since the time we shared together at my father's house; once a long time ago, at a party in 1988, and then again about a year and a half prior to this meeting, at my half-brother Curtis's 40th birthday celebration dinner.

During the time spent as adolescents in my father's house, we weren't very close or talkative at all. She was even more quiet and withdrawn than I was, even though she was four years my senior. Plus, having not too long come from Jamaica, academically and otherwise she had still been adjusting to being in England. What with this and her being even more shy and insecure than me, as a child with little sense of self, let alone self-esteem, I soon found myself caught up in a certain sibling rivalry; a one-upmanship with her that my father also seemed to encourage.

He used to set us tasks and encourage us to make good use of our time in whichever ways we could. I was into dancing and gymnastics at the time, so my creations were always in that vein, whereas Karen would reluctantly do a piece of academic work. Then, we would have to show him what we had done. I always felt like I had outshined her, which made me happy, as at last there was somebody I could outshine; that I was not in the shadow of.

The tables had turned. At my mother's house, I had been the one in Karen's shoes, and so she and I were never close, although there were times when I wished that we were. We just kept out of each other's way and got on with what we were getting on with, which I guess was essentially the business of survival.

However, there were also times when we, father included, used to play cards and other games together. I liked those times, as on the whole they tended to be pretty relaxed, and I also loved the cakes that Karen used to bake. Once, I tried to do the same, but ended up making a big, awful and totally inedible mess. I didn't dislike Karen, but I do wish that I had known and had liked her better, and her me, what with her being my older sister. Anyway, this had been the gist of our relationship up to that point.

After I had finished speaking, and she had listened and heard what I had to say, she went on to share her own experiences with our father. She shared how, for the slightest or even no apparent reason, he had beaten her almost daily, and sometimes more than once a day. She also shared how he had stolen from her, especially when, at sixteen, she had gotten her first job. She shared how he would take her wages and leave her literally penniless.

She shared how he manipulated her and had also done a similar act on her that I had vague memories of him having done to me. She also shared that on the first day of her arrival from Jamaica, he had said something sexually inappropriate to her She shared with me how his saying that had hurt her heart and had sunk it, especially with it having been said upon her arrival, making her fear what was to come. She was just fifteen years old at the time.

She also spoke about how he would ridicule and humiliate her in front of his friends and girlfriends, and shared how one of his friends had, on one such occasion, taken her aside and tried to speak some encouraging words to her, trying to show and make her know that how her father treated her was wrong, although that was all he did.

She shared how she was witness to how, one by one, he set about pursuing, seducing and eventually tearing down his women, affirming what he had previously shared with me. She remembered in particular one such woman, a beautiful Trinidadian who had been a lawyer at the time, but by the time he had finished with her, she was good for nothing, and a druggie to boot.

Karen also shared that, in regard to actual paternity, she had definitely once clearly heard our father say to his friend that he didn't think I was his daughter; that he had serious doubts. This was something I had wondered before, not only after what he had said when he and I had that talk about him finding out he was my father, but also because paternity was purely decided upon by resemblance.

At the end of the conversation, Karen looked me straight in the eyes and we sat in silence for a little while, very much both close to tears. After the silence was broken, she told me that she believed me, that she was there for me and would support me in whatever way I decided to go on from there.

The whole meeting felt so poignant, so real and of great comfort. I had felt such validation. It also felt like I had come home in my suspicions and memories of my father having sexually abused me; it felt like my body sighed with relief and rose up in that moment in the total joy of acknowledgement and the final release, of the missing piece.

When the talk was over, I went with Karen to pick up her son from preschool and stayed with her while she did her grocery shop, spending more time generally catching up on our overall lives. When we said our goodbyes, after she dropped me off at the station, I got on the train knowing in my heart that a corner had been turned, and that things would never again be the same. ***Everything had changed***.

When I got home, one of the first things I did was call my mother and share with her all that had taken place; all that I was finally clear on and decided about regarding my father's sexual abuse of me. I asked her if she was sure that he was indeed my dad. In fact, that was the first thing I asked her, which led into the rest.

Her reaction?

Even though to an extent she was understanding and happy that I had found Karen, and was able to bring and share my concerns and have them validated and confirmed, she still, even at that juncture, wasn't open to having an up front and honest conversation with me. She wasn't open to, by way of her past relationship with my dad and the paternity matter at hand, being brought into question. As far as she was concerned, he was lying; he was my father and that was the end of that.

When I tried to push further for a discussion by asking what age I was at this or that particular time, she still wasn't having any of it; she still wasn't open to that kind of honest communication. She still couldn't move herself out of the way enough to just be there for me, for once, which drove me to despair and made me, in that moment, absolutely fucking mad. It sent me into a certain rage, as I couldn't understand the why of it. If ever there was a time for a heart to heart, this was it!

Why wouldn't she hear me? Why, at this very difficult, corner-turning and totally life-transforming time in my life, wouldn't she *hear me* and come through *for me* in that hour of need? It made me feel crazy! It dumbstruck me, because it was like, even in this instant, she was giving the impression that I was making a big deal of nothing. Wasn't it a big deal? I couldn't continue the conversation, as I soon had to pick Julian up from school.

The next day, when I tried to broach the subject of the past and of the pain again, I was left further dumbstruck and enraged; enraged and thinking, *Here I am, sharing with her, my mother, that my father sexually abused me – my own father!* I wanted to ask questions, expecting her as mother to support me in this and in my putting together of the pieces, but she wouldn't have it.

Not only would she not have it, but in her old way of defensively blocking me, it and the subject out with her ranting and ravings, she tried to turn it all the way back around onto me, saying, asking and pleading, 'When are you going to drop all this?' 'How long are you going to bring all these things up and keep going over the past?' 'You're nearly forty now. Why can't you have some compassion for me?'

I totally lost it then. I felt the total craziness, desperation, unreasonableness and insanity of it all, and I screamed at her, 'Why can't you hear me? Why can't you listen to me? What about compassion for me? I'm here dying, for Christ's sake! And flung the phone down, so fucking devastated, but at the same time noting that the screaming had felt extremely and good. That scream had been a very, very, very long time coming…

In the weeks and months that followed, ***the need to scream*** remained with me as I endeavoured to come to terms with my father's abuse. The therapy group was a great source of support, as usual, helping me to feel and come to terms with the magnitude of feelings that washed over me from one moment to the next every day.

In the beginning, there was this numbness, shock and disbelief. The numbness didn't know if it wanted to 'feel' about the abuse, or if it could and even whether it should. Feelings of disbelief also followed; disbelief that the sexual abuse by my father really happened. The memories were so fragmented and scanty that at times I could not stop myself from questioning them. *What if I'm mixing and making this all up?* I thought. *What if I am getting it all wrong and making of him a victim instead?*

Sometimes, it was really hard keeping in touch with reality; with the everything in me that knew, and was coming to know again, what he had done. It was so hard believing in myself and feeling worthy of my own indignation, and the proverbial 'sweep it all under the carpet' conditioning, though somewhat more in the distance, began to tempt me again. Only in the group did I feel totally believed and entitled.

Everything had changed. That conviction played over and over again in my mind, and in my journals, mantra style. I didn't and couldn't see what the future would now hold for me, but I knew things would be different; that my whole world would never again be the same, knowing all that I know.

Then, there was the anger that never went. Even within the mixed feelings and the disbelieving, the anger had me doing, saying and making all the right moves, especially in the

beginning. In the days after speaking with Karen, I called up my
father on the phone first thing in the morning; the day before I
had only managed to get through to his answer phone. When he
picked up, the following conversation ensued, upon completion
of which I had immediately recorded the dialogue in my journal,
as I didn't want to lose any of it to unconsciousness:

I know about the sexual abuse, I begin.

What do you mean?

I know you sexually abused me.

When?

When I was a child… and you sexually abused Karen, too.

I didn't, he denies.

You physically beat her up, too.

All children get beaten from time to time, he rationalises.

You beat her up for any and everything. That's abuse.

At this point, he begins to get irritated. *Who's this?* he asks.

Marcia.

These things need to be spoken about face to face he says.

I only want to speak to you on the phone, I respond.

He begins to get angry. *All this is nonsense! Rubbish!*

He hangs up, and I call again and leave a message.

I'm shaming the devil, I tell him. *Mummy knows. Shame on you!*

Surprisingly, he didn't get as angry as I know he's capable of becoming, and as I had anticipated, and a part of me had feared. All that day, and for many days to come, I fought a great desire to telephone him day and night and terrorise the hell out of him.

A couple of weeks later, I called him again, ready to leave another message on his answer machine, as I didn't want him to be relaxing in his life while mine was in such turmoil; I didn't want him thinking that he was off the hook, or anything of the sort. Anyway, he answered on me, and another conversation ensued, which I had once again been keen to record.

Hello, it's me, Marcia, I say rather coolly, as he has taken me off guard slightly by picking up the phone.

Oh, Marcia, he says hesitantly, not knowing what to expect or what stance to take.

I think we need to talk about your sexual abuse of me, I say, thinking it best to be absolutely straight and direct.

He immediately starts to get agitated, but not too much. *I don't need to talk about all this silliness,* he says, making an effort to keep his cool.

Well, I think we need to talk about it, I reply, continuing to hold close to a growing inner strength, authority and self-confidence.

Listen, I don't need to talk about or go over all this silliness and nonsense. Besides, everything's changed now. If you need to talk, go talk to somebody'

I am talking about it in therapy, but I still think we need to talk.

He stops talking, so I end the conversation by saying:

OK, there's nothing else to say. I'll talk to Uncle Gordon instead.

I am resorting to blackmail at this point, trying to get him to budge, but he doesn't. I hang up.

Not too long after the above conversation, it begins to dawn on me that my father is never going to give me the confession; the truth that I so desperately at that time needed, if only to fully remember and recover all the memories of his abuse of me. I had wanted him to dig deep, and for the last, and perhaps first, time be the father I had needed. I soon came to the conclusion that I had to let go of that particular hope and dream and move on with my life, trusting and knowing that what I already knew, remembered and felt in my heart and soul was more than enough to go on with and begin a more complete healing from.

As the weeks passed, more impressions and flashbacks of his abuse resurfaced before disappearing as quickly as they'd come, which I had found, at the best of times, a great frustration because I so wanted to hold onto them long enough to record them. However, I reconciled that this was the best that my soul could do, and that the abused in me would, and perhaps could, manage and allow. So, in the midst of all of this, I wrote my father the following letter, for closure:

FATHER

For a time when you first came into my life, I was so happy to have a dad, even though it did take some getting used to. Having a father made me feel so special and made up for a lot of things that was already terribly missing and lacking. But it came to pass that you didn't really have any love in your heart for me. I was just pawn, a tool, a means to some devious end. So it wasn't long before you BETRAYED me: betrayed in a way that left great big gaping holes in my soul that I am still recovering from; and probably will be for the rest of my days.

I don't believe that you have faced the magnitude of your crime against me; against life. You took advantage of a poor, defenceless, vulnerable and needy child. How sick does that make you? You who like to go around 'JUDGING' people; being like judge and jury, acting like a 'doctor,' giving with one hand, destroying with the other. How SICK does that make you?!

I am filled with such rage for what you did to me. You sexually abused me, and emotionally and verbally too. I remember. You also took great pleasure in bringing down women. You hated women so much. I HATE YOU so much right now. You stole my innocence-what little that was left of it. How do you sleep? How do you live with yourself?

For a long time, and because somewhere deep inside I still needed your love and approval, I put what you did to me way back, out of my mind. But that had meant continuing to have emotionally and sexually abusive relationships with men: but not anymore. I have been talking to Karen and you did the same to her, but you also added beating her up into the mix. How could you do those things? I SO DESPISE YOU.

The least you could do is confess and take full responsibility, and give me a heartfelt apology. That's the least you can do. Until you are able to do this, I never want to hear from you again.

Your daughter,

Marcia.

I deliberately signed it 'your daughter,' because he did what he did despite what I am supposed to mean to him. I wanted that to resonate.

I shared the letter with the group the following week. It was all very emotional, deeply healing, liberating and releasing; releasing him and the hold I had continued to allow him to have over me. To this date, I have had no response from or contact with him, though I heard through the grapevine once that he was trying to discredit and defame my character, suggesting to my half-brother Curtis's ex-girlfriend that I'm not quite all there mentally.

When she had shared this with me, it had made me so angry. I really wanted to do him something, but soon calmed myself down and found the courage to share with her what was really going down. She went on to say that of course she never believed him, and every time in the conversation he had tried to discredit me, she instinctively and deliberately had gone out of her way to sing my praises.

Anyway, after the initial numbness, disbelief, confusion, anger and rage, I found myself at a place of deep sadness, grief and intense vulnerability. It was the vulnerability that I found the most difficult to deal with, as it brought within its midst equally intense moments of panic and acute anxiety, so much so that I came to be affected by ongoing palpitations and feeling faint, which lasted for some months before the heightened feelings and anxiety calmed down.

The palpitations had been a very scary experience for me, because it had felt like having an extra heartbeat right in centre of my chest, fluttering, like a butterfly, continuously; then at other times the sensation in my chest felt like a weighted and pained conglomerate enmeshment. A part of me was terrified for having spoken out and told. I truly felt broken-and ***broken-open,*** the kind broken Open Elizabeth Lesser speaks about in her book so entitled.

Emotionally and psychologically, I felt both extraordinarily fragile, and new. I felt like a tiny pink fleshy embryonic mesh and mess of a thing, which I had dreamt about around that time, having to hold in the palm of my hand. Of having to hold that budding new life, most gingerly, fearful I was of inadvertently squashing the life out of it, before it has had a chance to fully live.

During this healing time, it felt like I had given birth to myself; that I had psychologically gone back to my very beginning of time and recovered myself from the point of embryo; that is how deep the healing felt. A split off part of me needed incubating; needed space and time to more optimally develop and grow in (now) a safe, nourishing and facilitating environment.

There was that part of me, and the overall more vulnerable side of me, states of being that I was not at all familiar with and hadn't wanted to know as they terrified and haunted me: them and their repetitive tugging, needing, and wanting; them and their unmet dependency needs that I had been left way too early to meet, not being developmentally and psychologically equip. All that I could do at that tender age, was to try and distract my needy baby self, by keeping it sweet with all manner of substituted things, past and present.

I was actively in what has been called, a *Spiritual Emergency*, similar to- though much further along and at a deeper level- my first mental health breakdown/break through when I was with

Ronald. It was quite unnerving meeting and integrating this level of vulnerability and fragility into my total being, which had seen me making quite a number of visits to my local GP to seek some kind of remedy for a generalised anxiety these archaic feelings gravely afforded me then.

But, of course, **there was nothing wrong with me; shit had happened to me**, and the intensity of feelings I was experiencing was/is all part and parcel of my healing and enfoldment, which is also an aspect of the lifelong maturation process I had opened myself up to when I signed up for on this Journey **Back To Love.**

The only way out, was indeed *through*; to breathe and be and bear the delivery and arrival of a more real, whole and complete me, and in so doing discover **strength in vulnerability**. It was time to let into my total being the scarred-face girl who had once scared me in a dream some time ago...

This dream I had had early in my recovery journey and in it this scarred-face girl had come up to my living-room window, from outside, wanting me to let her in. In the dream she had absolutely terrified me, especially her scar and where it was located. She looked like she had truly been through **something**, a great big scary wounding something that I wanted nothing to do with, so I pushed her away from the window, back into the night. I didn't want trouble...

At times, the whole experience of the intense heart-brokenness and vulnerability had me even fearing leaving the house, in case I lost control and fainted or something, and in front of people, making a complete spectacle of myself. I felt very much alone at this time; alone in a big, wide, uncaring world of a time gone by. However, at the same time, I was very much in a different place with it all; an *'everything has changed and will never be the same' inner growing unfamiliar space*.

During this time, as a retreat of sorts, I took time out from the world of relationships with extended family, as well as friends, as part of the self-protective incubation process. I felt, and had received word in a dream, that for my own psychological growth and recovery, I should do so, which had felt both right and wrong at the same time, though mostly right.

It had felt so out of character not turning up at family gatherings as well as declining requests to meet up with friends; I didn't even have the energy for it. I couldn't imagine how I would be with my mother, and others, anymore. I wasn't the same and did not yet feel self-secure in this newer, more open, more vulnerable, more integrated me. I needed to fully find the strength in this new life position, and I had to do it on my own, or at the very least, with others who could better support me, and in that regard, I was still very much searching.

So, I kept a good and safe distance for a period of time, which had meant for me a very quiet Christmas 2004 and a sombre New Year's, not to mention a very lonely and quite depressing fortieth birthday in January. At forty, it very much felt and seemed that life was truly beginning for me, as much as an old maladaptive conditioned part of me was letting that be, having served its purpose of helping me survive until such time that I may truly thrive.

And as Spring approached, a growing calm began to make its

presence more felt. Then I had a poignant dream telling me it is time to write my life story. So, I took the decision to start working on **Back to Love**, fearing every step of the way whether it would come to full fruition; fearing whether the whole of me would allow it or if something would go wrong; whether I'd have the "stay with" power, or courage even to fully give to this endeavour, without giving up. It was quite a story, I knew. It had been quite a journey.

I was also worried that it would totally exhaust me and take me to places that I couldn't come back from. But I knew that they were all just fears and that fears have always been a part of the journey, and more than likely would continue to be as I stretched, reached, climbed, grew and leave what is past and no longer serve me way behind.

That was the key motivation behind writing **Back to Love**, along with a desire to give back to the world what it had given me, though now transformed and of good and better use to others in need; to others in need and making similar life-changing, corner-turning and dream-making decisions and journeys. So I focused on that; on conceiving, incubating, developing, and growing my brain-child book, taking it all the way through to delivery, and beyond, unspoiled and untouched, like how I first made my entry into the world..

Afterword

Dreams have always been a part of my journey, as places where I have received very important reassurances, ways forward and counsel. As such, I leave two key dreams with you that I feel fit this whole journey and where it now finds me, resting, momentarily, and waiting to receive word of the next step; what with this path being more like a spiral than it is a straight line, where, if we are open, we continually **keep coming back** to things we think we have understood, only to re-discover even deeper truths…only to rediscover the limitlessness of what we might be-come.

The first dream I had a few weeks before I was due to start the therapy group, following the Norman experience; the second dream I had just before the time I had made the premature decision to leave the group. I also include a List Poem entitled *Transitions*, which won me prize during these actively healing and self-rediscovery times, a poem, which to my mind, epitomises the journey from womb to tomb, and beyond.

Monday, 29ᵗʰ May 2000

Me, my sisters Lauren and Terri, as well as my dad, are somewhere in Oldhill Street, a road near where we used to live. The dream is about my dad sexually abusing me. I have proof of what he did, written on this skin-like stretchy material, but somehow water gets on it, and the evidence rubs off and disappears. Now, I don't have any proof. I am disappointed and upset, and once again go back to feeling isolated and alone. The dream ends.

Saturday, 29th March 2003

I am with the therapy group. The setting is a bit different than usual, illuminated brightly. Not many of the group members are there – maybe just one other. The members are more like invisible presences, rather than representing anyone in particular. The same applies to Anna, the group facilitator. The other person present is this man who is lying down beside me. He and I are together in this reverie of time having stood still.

In this reverie, it happens to be the last group session ever, and he and I are close, intimate, locked into this extraordinary, all-encompassing, sweet surrendered embrace together. I believe we are lying down, with me enveloping him and him me. He is taller than me, and it feels real comforting and reassuring to have him hold and embrace me in this way. I feel so real, at peace, fulfilled, cosy and warm. I feel *so* loved.

Then, it's the end of the group; the embrace. I am beginning to come out of the reverie. Everyone else has gone; the visible and invisible presences alike, and the facilitator has left a letter, a testimony of her impressions of me and of my life, both outside and within my group work experience. It is written on paper shaped like a love heart, and I am happy to have something concrete and tangible to take away with me. At the end of the letter, it says something like, 'Specially for you,' giving me the impression it's just for me, which makes me feel singled out and special. It is some kind of leaving present.

Then, I am even more awake and consciously aware. I am walking on this rich, shiny black and newly-laid tarmac; a foundation that acts as a bridge between my leaving the group and going someplace new. Under the bridge is a lake, and as I begin to walk across this beautiful, rich, newly-laid tarmac bridge, I realise it's a little way across to get to what I want; to where I want to and have to be.

I begin to also feel a bit nervous, doubtful and scared, which almost takes me to an emotional crossroads, where I have to decide whether I will give into fear; fear that the surface will not hold me up; will not be strong enough and I will end up falling into the water below and drowning, or something like that. The only other option is to instead have trust and faith in the strength of the new foundation, and step by step make my way across. I decide, almost immediately, to go with trust and faith.

As I am nearing the other side, there's this unknown woman also crossing the bridge, walking towards me, and I once again experience some panic regarding which way I should go, wondering if I should move out of the way and let her walk on the inside, where I am only just finding my feet. Once again, there is the fear that if I move out the way and let her pass, I might lose my footing and fall into the water below.

I need to make another quick, spontaneous decision, and I decide to stay on the inside, where I already am and where I have somehow received word is safe; the place to be and go. I am also given the impression that I should allow the woman to figure and navigate her own way across to the side I have just come from; that in effect, there is enough space on the bridge for us both without either of us falling, even if we are going in opposite directions.

I manage to get across and I am feeling OK; very well, in fact.

Then, I go to walk down a road, only to discover that it is cordoned off by a long lorry, guarded and assisted by government officials. Apparently, some man has just raped a woman or something of that sort. The scene looks like a war scene. It becomes a little sketchy at this point, but anyway, it turns out that I could hold some crucial information to ensure the culprit's arrest.

I am surprised at how easily and willingly I decide to cooperate and speak the truth. I tell them all that I know; it all just flows. While I am telling them what I know, the culprit's face comes to mind: a white, bald, middle-aged man, looking, or trying to look, menacing; a Freddie Kruger look-alike. A thought also crosses my mind of what if he comes after me for telling, but I don't let the thought stop me; I continue to talk. It's like I have confidence and faith that he will be brought to justice and will not be a threat to me anymore. As I talk and talk, the image of him recedes and ceases to threaten me.

While talking away, I am amazed at my expressiveness; of the wholeness and completeness of the story I am sharing; how articulate, thorough, clear and concise my vocabulary and speech is. When I am finally and thoroughly through, the unknown official man who I am speaking to says words to the effects of, 'Wow! That's a book!' He seems satisfied; he now has more than enough to go on. The dream ends.

A List Poem

Transitions

New Old Soul

Passage

Dark Safe Warm

Joy Waters Life

Body

Breath Lights Time

Sweet Peace Serenity

Rampant

Emotions Waves Frustrations

Fearful Waiting Wanting

Conditions

Gratification Comforts Yearnings

Hope Plays Imagination

Trusting

Fun Loving Faith

Exploratory Independent Discovery

Self

Sexual Sensual Pleasures

Artistic Creative Expressions

Spirit

Intuition Whispers Voices

Instinctual Inner Learnings

Pure

True Wholesome Relations

Seasons Breeze Infinity

Free

Me Two We

One

EPILOGUE

"It's never too late to be what you might have been."
George Eliot

Today I am nothing like I was. I was a very quiet child growing up, for all the reasons shared in this story; I was quiet and shy with an ever ready plastered on smile that hid how I truly

felt inside. I became so very quiet I almost successfully made myself invisible. I got so good at being quiet that even when I needed to tell, I couldn't find the words: they too like me were no-where to be found. I suffered in silence-a godsend to (my) abusers.

But the buck stopped with me-and not accidentally, but by choice. By a choice I made when I became a mother, therefore automatically a teacher. Back then I promised myself to make a difference. A promise that continues to date, in whatever ***ripe for right-doing*** situation I may find myself.

It has been words that have saved me; searching for them and sharing them in therapy, through journaling, poems, and writing my life story, hoping one day it will be published. I love words, they help me to have a say-to have **MY** say. They help me to not be quiet about the things, that left unspoken, like cancer, left untreated, kills. So The Word here is*:*

There Is Freedom, Healing and Power In The Tongue- and In Its Expression.

On this ***Back to Love*** self-re-discovery journey, I have come to believe that our reason for being here, on this earth plane, is to live and be more self-knowing and loving human beings. This is a way of being that doesn't magically and automatically spring forth from within us of its own accord, even though as children we have that pure Spirit and Potential in greater abundance. That same Spirit and Potential are still within us as adults, open to being nourished and truly raised up if we allow it.

Being human is, for me, a way of being that absolutely needs the good, wholesome relations of other fellow human beings to help keep and heed the budding human spirit towards those more life- and love-affirming means and ends. For me, this is something we should be learning about in schools. I believe that such an education would make individual life purposes fall much better into place, minimising individual, social and community dis-ease and unrest.

As John Bradshaw reminds us in his book, *Homecoming: Reclaiming and Championing Your Inner Child*:

Children are naturally predisposed to love and affection. However, the child must first be loved before he can love.

In the same book, Bradshaw quotes from Ashley Montagu's *Growing Young*:

Of all humanising need; beyond all others it (love) makes us human.

Love may not be *all* that we need, but it does seem to make a great big qualitative life experience difference, especially, and also in particular regard, to our personal and collective well-being and continued existence, as we ourselves, as species, are in danger of extinction. So, let us not for a moment longer continue to abandon the need to be Real Life, One Life, human beings, and in that becoming walk a certain path; the path we learn to walk with Heart.

In so doing and being, let us also learn to walk by faith and not solely by sight, lest we lose sight of the much bigger picture, that ***we all are in this world together***, so we ought to learn how to love one another. We cannot live in a house and believe that what is happening in other unconscious and occupied rooms of the house will not spill out and negatively impact and pollute the whole house/life experience…We are all impacted by injustice.

Let us get back to the basics, back to love, to the sturdy foundation of self/love, and on that ground build and become all that we might be, personally and collectively. It is possible to create conditions that supports and favours win-win situations; we have that creativity & possibility within us, to create environs where we all can win!

I hope that the little difference I can make, within these pages, will go a very long way, for the greater good. That's how I choose to work my unfinished business out, and in so doing sing the particular truth song that I believe my soul came to this Earthplane to share, sing, and have heard.

I hope the sharing of my life story has provided you with some of the manna that the heart and soul needs to go on, and in so doing release, the 'all manner of things' once needed for survival, but no longer serves us now. It has been a soulful, joyful, pleasure sharing my journey with you, and telling my story. Thank you so very much for listening, and in this time, in this moment, baring down and receiving the delivery of ***Back To Love*** with me!

Godspeed on your Journeys and your own eminent *Bundles of Peace & Joy*, in whatever creative and authentic forms they Come Into Being!

Love & Light,

Denise Marcia James, May 2020

P.S. And she *Lived*, self-knowingly & self-lovingly ever after.

Denise James

CPSIA information can be obtained
at www.ICGtesting.com
Printed in the USA
LVHW021217121120
671417LV00014B/1952